100 meals in minutes

THE AUSTRALIAN Women's Weekly

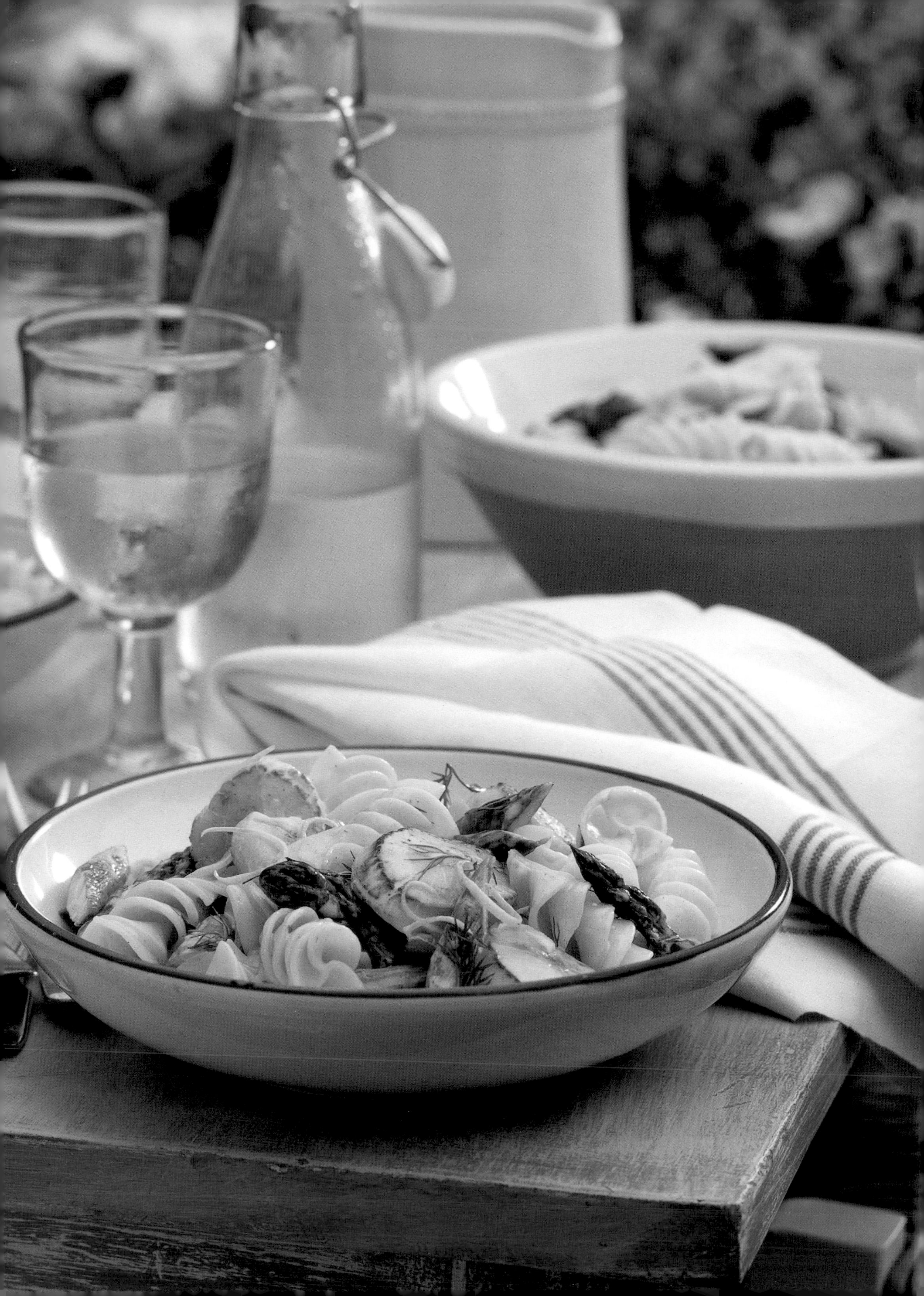

contents

We all want to give our family, friends and ourselves, the best food possible in the most efficient time. After a busy day, there is nothing better than coming home, knowing that you can have some great food on the table without spending hours in the kitchen. Build up a clever store cupboard of herbs, spices and dried or bottled ingredients you can add to zest up the flavour. Cooking these meals won't take you hours in the kitchen, but they will certainly taste as though you have!

Food Director

Pamela Clark

starters

carpaccio with fresh herbs

500g piece of beef eye-fillet, about 6cm diameter
⅓ cup (80ml) extra virgin olive oil
¼ cup (60ml) lemon juice
¼ cup firmly packed fresh basil
¼ cup firmly packed fresh flat-leaf parsley
1 tablespoon fresh oregano
1 tablespoon coarsely chopped fresh chives
¼ cup (25g) drained sun-dried tomatoes, sliced thinly
2 tablespoons flaked parmesan cheese
freshly ground black pepper

1 Remove any excess fat from beef. Wrap beef tightly in cling film; freeze about 1½ hours or until partly frozen.
2 Cut beef into 1mm slices; freeze until required.
3 Just before serving, place beef on serving plate. Drizzle with oil and juice; top with combined herbs, tomato, cheese and pepper.

on the table in 25 minutes (plus freezing time)
serves 8
per serving 12.9g fat; 747kJ (178 cal)
tips Sashimi-quality tuna can be used in place of the beef; ask the fishmonger to slice it paper-thin for you.
Omit the parmesan and add a sprinkling of baby capers.

bagna cauda

2⅔ cups (600ml) whipping cream
60g butter
45g can anchovy fillets, drained, chopped finely
2 cloves garlic, crushed

1 Place cream in small saucepan; bring to a boil. Reduce heat to low; simmer, uncovered, about 15 minutes or until cream thickens, stirring frequently.
2 Meanwhile, melt butter over low heat in medium saucepan, taking care not to brown butter. Add anchovy and garlic; stir until mixture is blended well and becomes paste-like.
3 Stir hot cream into anchovy mixture until well combined; serve warm.

on the table in 25 minutes
makes 2¾ cups
per tablespoon 9.5g fat; 370kJ (88 cal)
tip Traditionally served warm, you can serve bagna cauda in a fondue pot with a small tea light or gentle flame underneath. Serve with your favourite selection of crisp vegetables.

baked mushrooms

9 medium flat mushrooms (900g)
60g butter, melted
3 bacon rashers (210g), chopped finely
4 spring onions, chopped finely
2 cloves garlic, crushed
2 tablespoons stale breadcrumbs
1 tablespoon cream
2 teaspoons fresh oregano, chopped coarsely
2 tablespoons grated parmesan

1 Gently remove stalks from eight of the mushrooms. Finely chop stalks and remaining mushroom.
2 Brush mushroom caps all over with butter. Place on lightly greased oven trays.
3 Cook bacon and onion in small non-stick frying pan until bacon is crisp. Add chopped mushroom, garlic and breadcrumbs. Cook, stirring, until well combined. Remove from heat; stir in cream, oregano and cheese. Divide bacon mixture between mushroom caps.
4 Bake in moderately hot oven about 10 minutes or until hot.

on the table in 25 minutes
serves 4
per serving 17.4g fat; 990kJ (236 cal)
tip Cap mushrooms can be substituted for the flat mushrooms. Cook 5 minutes; cool slightly before serving.

baked mussels

24 small black mussels (500g)
¾ cup (180ml) water
¼ cup (60ml) olive oil
1 clove garlic, crushed
2 tablespoons finely chopped fresh parsley
½ cup (35g) stale breadcrumbs
1 medium tomato (130g), deseeded, chopped finely

1 Scrub mussels, remove beards. Heat the water in large saucepan. Cook mussels in the water, covered, over high heat about 3 minutes or until shells open. Drain; discard liquid.
2 Loosen mussels; remove from shell. Discard half of each shell; reserve half. Combine mussel meat, oil, garlic, parsley and breadcrumbs in small bowl; mix well. Cover; refrigerate 30 minutes.
3 Place one mussel in each half shell; place on oven tray. Combine tomato with remaining breadcrumb mixture; spoon over mussels. Bake in hot oven about 5 minutes or until breadcrumbs are browned lightly.

on the table in 30 minutes (plus marinating time)
serves 4
per serving 14.5g fat; 738kJ (716 cal)

chilli scallops

1 tablespoon groundnut oil
32 small scallops
4 cloves garlic, sliced thinly
50g fresh ginger, peeled, sliced thinly
2 fresh red thai chillies, deseeded, chopped finely
3 spring onions, sliced thinly
⅓ cup (80ml) sweet chilli sauce
1 teaspoon fish sauce
2 teaspoons brown sugar
½ cup (125ml) chicken stock
¼ cup loosely packed, chopped fresh coriander

1 Heat half of the oil in wok or large frying pan; stir-fry scallops, iin batches, until just changed in colour.
2 Heat remaining oil in wok; stir-fry garlic, ginger, chilli and onion until onion is soft.
3 Stir in combined sauces, sugar and stock; bring to a boil. Return scallops to wok; stir until heated through. Serve scallops sprinkled with coriander.

on the table in 30 minutes
serves 4
per serving 6.1g fat; 585kJ (140 cal)
tips We used scallops with roe attached but the roe can be left out if you prefer. If you buy scallops in their shell, don't discard the shell, they are great (washed and dried) to use as serving dishes.
You will need a piece of ginger about 5cm long for this recipe.

roast pepper & prosciutto bruschetta

½ loaf ciabatta (275g)
3 cloves garlic, halved
¼ cup (60ml) olive oil
2 medium red peppers (400g)
5 prosciutto slices (75g), chopped coarsely
1 tablespoon balsamic vinegar
2 tablespoons fresh oregano

1 Cut ciabatta into 1.5cm thick slices; halve any large slices crossways. Toast under hot grill until browned lightly; while still hot, rub one side of toast with garlic. Place toast in single layer on tray; drizzle oil evenly over toast.
2 Quarter peppers; remove and discard seeds and membranes. Place pepper on oven tray; roast under hot grill or in very hot oven, skin-side up, until skin blisters and blackens. Cover pepper pieces in plastic 5 minutes. Peel away skin; discard. Cut pepper into thin strips.
3 Cook prosciutto in medium heated non-stick frying pan until crisp. Add pepper and vinegar to pan; stir to combine. Cool to room temperature.
4 Just before serving divide pepper mixture among bruschetta; top with oregano.

on the table in 27 minutes
serves 8
per serving 8.4g fat; 695kJ (166 cal)

creamy mushroom bruschetta

½ loaf ciabatta (275g)
4 cloves garlic, halved
½ cup (125ml) olive oil
250g flat mushrooms, chopped finely
1 tablespoon lemon juice
½ cup (125ml) cream
125g button mushrooms, sliced thinly
2 tablespoons finely grated parmesan
¼ cup coarsely chopped fresh chives

1 Cut ciabatta into 1.5cm thick slices; halve any large slices crossways. Toast under hot grill until browned lightly; while still hot, rub one side of toast with three cloves of the garlic. Place toast in single layer on tray; drizzle half of the oil evenly over toast.
2 Crush remaining garlic. Heat remaining oil in medium non-stick frying pan; cook flat mushrooms, stirring over heat, until very soft. Add juice; stir over high heat until absorbed. Pour in cream; stir to combine. Gently stir in button mushrooms; stir over high heat until almost all liquid is absorbed. Remove from heat; stir in cheese.
3 Just before serving, top bruschetta with mushroom mixture; sprinkle with chives.

on the table in 35 minutes
serves 8
per serving 22.7g fat; 1221kJ (292 cal)

olive, anchovy & caper bruschetta

½ loaf ciabatta (275g)
3 cloves garlic, halved
⅓ cup (80ml) olive oil
3 anchovy fillets, drained, chopped finely
½ cup (60g) pitted black olives, chopped finely
1 tablespoon drained baby capers
1 tablespoon lemon juice
⅓ cup (25g) parmesan flakes
2 tablespoons marjoram

1 Cut ciabatta into 1.5cm thick slices; halve any large slices crossways. Toast under hot grill until browned lightly; while still hot, rub one side of toast with garlic. Place toast in single layer on tray; drizzle ¼ cup (60ml) of the oil evenly over toast.
2 Combine anchovy, olives, capers, juice and remaining oil in small bowl.
3 Just before serving, divide olive mixture among bruschetta; top with cheese then marjoram.

on the table in 20 minutes
serves 8
per serving 11.3g fat; 792kJ (189 cal)

tomato & rocket bruschetta

½ loaf ciabatta (275g)
3 cloves garlic, halved
¼ cup (60ml) olive oil
3 medium plum tomatoes (225g), chopped finely
½ small red onion (50g), chopped finely
25g baby rocket leaves

1 Cut ciabatta into 1.5cm thick slices; halve any large slices crossways. Toast under hot grill until browned lightly; while still hot, rub one side of toast with garlic. Place toast in single layer on tray; drizzle oil evenly over toast.
2 Combine tomato and onion in small bowl.
3 Just before serving, top bruschetta with tomato mixture, then rocket; sprinkle with freshly ground black pepper, if desired.

on the table in 20 minutes
serves 8
per serving 7.8g fat; 628kJ (150 cal)

tomatoes & goat's cheese in walnut dressing

8 medium vine-ripened tomatoes (1.5kg), sliced thickly
150g goat's cheese, sliced thickly
¼ cup (25g) walnuts, toasted, chopped coarsely
¼ cup (60ml) olive oil
1 clove garlic, crushed
1½ tablespoons raspberry vinegar
2 teaspoons dijon mustard
2 teaspoons coarsely chopped fresh thyme
2 teaspoons sugar

1 Place a slice of tomato on each serving plate; top with a slice of cheese.
2 Repeat, sprinkling nuts and combined remaining ingredients between layers.

on the table in 15 minutes
serves 6
per serving 18.5g fat; 938kJ (224 cal)
tips Hazelnuts can be substituted for walnuts in this recipe and, if you have hazelnut or walnut oil at hand, use one of these, rather than the olive oil.
Sample a few different goat's cheeses before you decide on one; they vary greatly in texture and taste.

prosciutto-wrapped haloumi

120g piece haloumi cheese
8 slices prosciutto
2 tablespoons chopped fresh flat-leaf parsley
1 teaspoon lemon juice

1 Cut cheese into eight fingers. Wrap each finger in a slice of prosciutto, securing ends with toothpicks.
2 Cook on heated oiled grill plate (or grill or barbecue) about 8 minutes or until browned all over. Serve sprinkled with parsley and juice.

on the table in 13 minutes
serves 4
per serving 7.6g fat; 531kJ (127 cal)

soups

green pea soup with mint pistou

1 tablespoon olive oil
1 small leek (200g), sliced thinly
1 clove garlic, crushed
2 large potatoes (600g), chopped coarsely
3 cups (360g) frozen peas
3 cups (750ml) water
2 cups (500ml) vegetable stock

mint pistou
2 cups loosely packed fresh mint leaves
¼ cup (20g) finely grated parmesan
1 tablespoon lemon juice
1 clove garlic, quartered
¼ cup (60ml) olive oil

1 Heat oil in large saucepan; cook leek and garlic, stirring, until leek softens. Add potato, peas, the water and stock; bring to a boil. Reduce heat; simmer, covered, about 10 minutes or until potato is tender. Cool 15 minutes.
2 Meanwhile, make mint pistou.
3 Blend or process soup, in batches, until smooth. Return soup to same cleaned pan; stir over medium heat until hot.
4 Serve bowls of soup topped with pistou.

mint pistou Blend or process ingredients until smooth.
on the table in 30 minutes (plus cooling time)
serves 4
per serving 20.9g fat; 1634kJ (391 cal)

chicken, corn & noodle chowder

1 medium (150g) brown onion, chopped coarsely
2 cloves garlic, crushed
420g can corn kernels, drained
750g can small potatoes, drained, quartered
1 litre (4 cups) chicken stock
375g chicken tenderloins, chopped coarsely
150g fresh egg noodles
2 tablespoons low-fat soured cream

1 Heat oiled large pan; cook onion and garlic, stirring, until onion softens. Add corn, potato and stock, bring to boil; simmer, covered, 10 minutes.
2 Blend or process potato mixture, in batches, until smooth. Return potato mixture to same pan, add chicken and noodles; simmer, uncovered, about 10 minutes or until chicken is tender.
3 Serve with soured cream, topped with finely sliced fresh herbs, if desired.

on the table in 30 minutes
serves 4
per serving 7.5g fat; 1469kJ (359 cal)

minted lamb & vermicelli soup

100g bean thread vermicelli
1 tablespoon groundnut oil
600g lamb fillets, sliced thinly
2 teaspoons bottled chopped chilli
2 tablespoons finely chopped fresh lemongrass
2 tablespoons grated fresh ginger
4 cloves garlic, crushed
⅓ cup (80ml) fish sauce
1.5 litres (6 cups) chicken stock
1 tablespoon sugar
500g asparagus, trimmed, chopped
¼ cup chopped fresh coriander leaves
⅓ cup chopped fresh mint leaves
8 spring onions, chopped finely
4 medium (760g) tomatoes, deseeded, sliced

1 Place vermicelli in large heatproof bowl, cover with boiling water, stand until just tender; drain.
2 Meanwhile, heat half of the oil in large pan; cook lamb, in batches, until browned all over.
3 Heat remaining oil in same pan; cook chilli, lemongrass, ginger and garlic, stirring, until fragrant. Add sauce, stock and sugar; cook, stirring, until mixture boils.
4 Add asparagus; simmer, uncovered, until asparagus is just tender. Add herbs, onion, tomato, vermicelli and lamb; stir until soup is hot.

on the table in 30 minutes
serves 6
per serving 11.7g fat; 1613kJ (385 cal)

tomato & borlotti bean soup

2 medium (300g) brown onions, chopped coarsely
2 cloves garlic, crushed
11 large (1kg) plum tomatoes, chopped coarsely
2 cups (500ml) chicken stock
1 tablespoon Worcestershire sauce
2 tablespoons finely chopped fresh parsley
2 x 400g cans borlotti beans, rinsed, drained

1 Heat oiled large pan; cook onion and garlic, stirring, until onion softens.
2 Stir in tomato; cook, stirring, about 3 minutes or until tomato softens. Add stock and sauce, bring to boil; simmer, covered, 15 minutes.
3 Blend or process tomato mixture, in batches, until almost smooth. Return tomato mixture to pan, stir in parsley and beans; simmer, uncovered, about 5 minutes or until hot.

on the table in 30 minutes
serves 4
per serving 0.8g fat; 417kJ (100 cal)

pumpkin soup

40g butter
1 large brown onion (200g), chopped coarsely
3 bacon rashers (210g), chopped coarsely
1.5kg pumpkin, chopped coarsely
2 large potatoes (600g), chopped coarsely
1.5 litres (6 cups) chicken stock

1 Melt butter in large saucepan; cook onion and bacon, stirring, until onion softens. Stir in pumpkin and potato.
2 Stir in stock, bring to a boil; simmer, uncovered, about 20 minutes or until pumpkin is soft.
3 Blend or process soup, in batches, until pureed. Return to same cleaned pan; stir until heated through.

on the table in 35 minutes
serves 6
per serving 8.3g fat; 1008kJ (241cal)
tip The smoothest consistency for this soup can be achieved by using a blender, stick blender or mouli.

chunky vegetable & pasta soup

1 tablespoon olive oil
2 medium brown onions (300g), chopped finely
2 cloves garlic, crushed
4 trimmed celery stalks (400g), chopped finely
2 medium carrots (240g), chopped finely
410g can tomato puree
⅓ cup (90g) tomato paste
420g can red kidney beans, rinsed, drained
3 litres (12 cups) chicken stock
500g penne pasta
¼ cup finely chopped fresh flat-leaf parsley

1 Heat oil in large saucepan, add onion, garlic, celery and carrot; cook, stirring, until onion softens.
2 Add tomato puree, paste, beans and stock; bring to a boil.
3 Add pasta; boil, uncovered, until pasta is tender. Serve sprinkled with parsley.

on the table in 35 minutes
serves 6
per serving 6.6g fat; 2011kJ (480 cal)
tip The pasta will absorb the liquid as it stands. If preparing ahead, more stock may need to be added on reheating.

tomato, pepper & butterbean soup

1 tablespoon olive oil
2 medium brown onions (300g), chopped coarsely
1 large red pepper (350g), chopped coarsely
1 medium fresh red chilli, chopped finely
810g can crushed tomatoes
1 litre (4 cups) chicken stock
2 x 300g cans butterbeans, rinsed, drained

1 Heat oil in large saucepan, add onion, pepper and chilli; cook, stirring, until vegetables are very soft. Add undrained tomatoes and stock; bring to a boil. Reduce heat; simmer, covered, about 15 minutes or until thickened slightly.
2 Blend or process soup until smooth; return to same cleaned pan. Add beans; stir until hot.
3 Serve soup with garlic bread, if desired.

on the table in 30 minutes
serves 6
per serving 6.5g fat; 698kJ (167 cal)
tips Cans labelled butterbeans are, in fact, cannellini beans.
In place of butterbeans, try kidney beans, chickpeas or small pasta, if desired.

asian mushroom broth

cooking-oil spray
4 spring onions, chopped finely
1 trimmed celery stalk (100g), chopped finely
1.5 litres (6 cups) chicken stock
1½ cups (375ml) water
¼ cup (60ml) light soy sauce
100g shiitake mushrooms, sliced thinly
100g enoki mushrooms, trimmed
150g oyster mushrooms, sliced thinly
150g chestnut mushrooms, sliced thinly
½ teaspoon five-spice powder
2 tablespoons finely chopped fresh garlic chives

1 Spray heated large saucepan with cooking-oil spray; cook onion and celery, stirring, until vegetables soften.
2 Add stock, the water and sauce; bring to a boil. Add mushrooms and five-spice; return to a boil. Reduce heat; simmer 2 minutes or until mushrooms soften.
3 Just before serving, sprinkle with chives.

on the table in 20 minutes
serves 4
per serving 2.7g fat; 372kJ (89 cal)
tip Other varieties of mushrooms, such as button or shimeji, can also be used in this recipe.

lentil & spinach soup

2 tablespoons groundnut oil
2 large brown onions (400g), chopped finely
2 cloves garlic, crushed
2 teaspoons ground cumin
1 teaspoon ground turmeric
1 teaspoon ground coriander
3 cups (600g) red lentils
1.25 litres (5 cups) chicken stock
1 litre (4 cups) water
500g spinach, trimmed, chopped finely

1 Heat oil in large saucepan; cook onion and garlic, stirring, until onion is soft. Add spices; cook, stirring, until fragrant.
2 Add lentils; stir to combine with spice mixture. Add stock and the water; bring to a boil. Simmer soup, uncovered, about 20 minutes or until lentils are tender.
3 Blend or process soup, in batches, until smooth. Return soup to same cleaned pan, add spinach; stir over heat until hot.

on the table in 35 minutes
serves 8
per serving 6.9g fat; 1122kJ (268 cal)

cream of courgette soup

30g butter
1 large brown onion (200g), chopped finely
2 cloves garlic, crushed
2 tablespoons plain flour
8 large courgettes (1.2kg), chopped coarsely
1½ cups (375ml) chicken stock
1 cup (250ml) water
½ cup (125ml) cream

1 Melt butter in large saucepan; cook onion and garlic, stirring, until onion softens. Stir in flour and courgettes; cook, stirring, 2 minutes.
2 Stir in stock and the water, bring to a boil; simmer, uncovered, about 15 minutes or until courgettes are tender.
3 Blend or process soup, in batches, until smooth.
4 Just before serving, return soup to same cleaned pan. Add cream; stir over medium heat until hot.
5 Serve soup topped with chervil, if desired.

on the table in 35 minutes
serves 4
per serving 19g fat; 1005kJ (240 cal)

tomato, corn & chilli chicken soup

2 tablespoons olive oil
340g chicken breast fillets
1 medium red onion (170g), chopped finely
1 tablespoon plain flour
1.5 litres (6 cups) chicken stock
2 cups (500ml) tomato juice
420g can corn kernels, drained
2 small fresh red thai chillies, deseeded, chopped finely
¼ cup loosely packed fresh coriander leaves

1 Heat half of the oil in large saucepan; cook chicken until cooked through. When cool enough to handle, shred chicken into small pieces.
2 Heat remaining oil in same pan; cook onion, stirring, until soft. Add flour; cook, stirring, until mixture bubbles and thickens. Gradually stir in stock and juice; cook, stirring, until mixture boils and thickens slightly.
3 Add chicken, corn and chilli; stir over heat until soup is hot. Just before serving, sprinkle with coriander.

on the table in 30 minutes
serves 6
per serving 8.5g fat; 1053kJ (252 cal)
tip A ready-cooked chicken can be substituted for the chicken breasts; discard skin, excess fat and all bones before shredding the meat.

rice & noodles

chilli prawn & noodle salad

250g medium cooked prawns
¼ cup (60ml) lime juice
2 tablespoons sweet chilli sauce
1 red Dutch chilli, deseeded, sliced
1 green Dutch chilli, deseeded, sliced
2 teaspoons sugar
200g bean thread noodles
2 tablespoons shredded fresh mint leaves

1 Shell and devein prawns, leaving tails intact. Combine prawns with juice, sauce, chillies and sugar in large bowl.

2 Place noodles in large heatproof bowl, cover with boiling water, stand until tender; drain.

3 Combine noodles and mint with prawn mixture.

on the table in 30 minutes
serves 4
per serving 1.4g fat; 887kJ (212 cal)
tip Red and green Thai chillies may be substituted for the Dutch chillies in this recipe.

fried rice with prawns

6 dried shiitake mushrooms
500g medium uncooked prawns
1 tablespoon groundnut oil
1 medium (150g) brown onion, sliced thinly
1 teaspoon sesame oil
1 clove garlic, crushed
1 tablespoon grated fresh ginger
1 medium (200g) red pepper, chopped coarsely
1 medium (120g) carrot, sliced thinly
2 sticks celery, sliced
100g mangetout
500g packet frozen pre-cooked rice
1 cup (80g) beansprouts
6 spring onions, sliced thinly
¼ cup (60ml) oyster sauce
¼ cup (60ml) hoisin sauce
1 tablespoon fish sauce

1 Place mushrooms in small heatproof bowl, cover with boiling water, stand 10 minutes; drain. Discard stems; slice caps finely. Shell and devein prawns, leaving tails intact.
2 Heat half the groundnut oil in wok or large pan; stir-fry brown onion until soft. Add sesame oil, garlic, ginger and prawns, stir-fry until prawns just change colour; remove from wok.
3 Heat remaining groundnut oil in wok, add pepper, carrot, celery and mangetout, stir-fry until vegetables are just tender. Return prawn mixture to wok with mushroom, rice, sprouts, spring onion and sauces; cook, stirring, until hot.

on the table in 30 minutes
serves 4
per serving 8.2g fat; 1537kJ (367 cal)
tip Instead of packaged pre-cooked rice, you can cook-ahead 2½ cups (500g) long-grain rice for this recipe. Spread cooked rice on tray, cover with absorbent paper; refrigerate overnight.

spicy chicken fried rice

2 teaspoons groundnut oil
2 eggs, lightly beaten
500g chicken thigh fillets, sliced thinly
2 medium (300g) brown onions, chopped finely
1 tablespoon ground cumin
2 teaspoons ground coriander
¼ teaspoon cardamom seeds
1 teaspoon ground cinnamon
2 bird's eye chillies, deseeded, chopped finely
2 cloves garlic, crushed
1 large (350g) red pepper, sliced thinly
115g fresh baby corn, halved lengthways
500g packet frozen pre-cooked rice
4 spring onions, sliced finely
2 tablespoons kecap manis
2 tablespoons coarsely chopped fresh coriander leaves

1 Heat ½ teaspoon of the oil in wok or large pan, add half the egg, swirl so egg forms a thin omelette; cook until set.
2 Transfer omelette to board, roll, cut into thin strips. Repeat with remaining egg and another ½ teaspoon oil.
3 Heat remaining oil in wok; stir-fry chicken and brown onion, in batches, until chicken is tender. Stir-fry spices, chillies and garlic in wok until fragrant. Add pepper and corn; stir-fry until just tender. Return chicken mixture to wok with omelette strips, rice, spring onion, kecap manis and coriander; stir-fry until hot.

on the table in 30 minutes
serves 4
per serving 11.9g fat; 1887kJ (451 cal)
tip Instead of packaged pre-cooked rice, you can cook-ahead 2½ cups (500g) long-grain rice for this recipe. Spread cooked rice on tray, cover with absorbent paper; refrigerate overnight.

pork, pine nut & cointreau risotto

500g pork fillets
1 tablespoon teriyaki marinade
1 teaspoon finely grated orange rind
3 cloves garlic, crushed
1 large (200g) brown onion, chopped finely
2 cups (400g) arborio rice
1.25 litres (5 cups) chicken stock
½ cup (125ml) dry white wine
2 tablespoons Cointreau
150g baby spinach leaves
2 tablespoons pine nuts, toasted
2 tablespoons coarsely chopped fresh lemon thyme

1 Place pork on rack in baking dish; brush with combined marinade and rind. Bake, uncovered, in hot oven 20 minutes. Cover pork, stand 5 minutes; slice thinly.
2 Meanwhile, cook garlic and onion in heated, oiled large pan, stirring, until onion softens. Add rice, stock, wine and Cointreau, bring to boil, simmer, covered, 15 minutes, stirring midway through cooking.
3 Remove from heat, stand, covered, 10 minutes. Gently stir in spinach, pine nuts, thyme and pork.

on the table in 30 minutes
serves 4
per serving 7.6g fat; 2572kJ (614 cal)

mushroom, spinach & lemon risotto

2 medium (300g) brown onions, chopped finely
3 cloves garlic, crushed
1 tablespoon finely grated lemon rind
300g button mushrooms, halved
2 cups (400g) arborio rice
1.5 litres (6 cups) chicken stock
1 cup (250ml) dry white wine
300g baby spinach leaves
2 tablespoons coarsely chopped fresh lemon thyme

1 Heat oiled large pan; cook onion, garlic, rind and mushrooms, stirring, until mushrooms are browned lightly.
2 Add rice, stock and wine, bring to boil; simmer, covered, 15 minutes, stirring midway through cooking.
3 Remove from heat; stand, covered, 10 minutes. Gently stir in spinach and lemon thyme.

on the table in 30 minutes
serves 4
per serving 1.6g fat; 1916kJ (458 cal)

sesame chicken noodle salad

680g chicken breast fillets, sliced
1 clove garlic, crushed
2 tablespoons sweet chilli sauce
½ teaspoon sesame oil
¼ cup (60ml) rice vinegar
2 tablespoons soy sauce
1 tablespoon lemon juice
1 spring onion, sliced finely
2 teaspoons sugar
600g fresh egg noodles
1 medium (200g) yellow pepper
1 large (180g) carrot
200g watercress, trimmed
1 tablespoon groundnut oil
250g asparagus, trimmed, halved
2 teaspoons sesame seeds, toasted

1 Combine chicken, garlic and chilli sauce in large bowl.
2 For dressing, combine sesame oil, vinegar, soy sauce, juice, onion and sugar in jar; shake well.
3 Cook noodles in large pan of boiling water, uncovered, until just tender; drain.
4 Discard seeds and membranes from pepper, cut pepper and carrot into long thin strips. Combine noodles, pepper, carrot and watercress in large serving bowl; mix well.
5 Heat groundnut oil in wok or large pan; stir-fry chicken mixture, in batches, until browned and tender. Add asparagus to wok, stir-fry until just tender.
6 Combine chicken and asparagus with noodle mixture, drizzle with dressing, sprinkle with seeds.

on the table in 30 minutes
serves 6
per serving 8g fat; 1410kJ (337 cal)

sweet soy chicken & noodles

250g soba noodles
1 tablespoon groundnut oil
600g chicken breast fillets, sliced
200g sugar snap peas
2 tablespoons sweet soy sauce
4 spring onions, sliced thinly
6 (200g) radishes, sliced thinly
2 tablespoons finely chopped fresh coriander leaves

1 Cook noodles in large pan of boiling water, uncovered, until just tender; drain. Rinse noodles under hot water; cover to keep warm.
2 Meanwhile, heat half the oil in wok or large pan; stir-fry chicken, in batches, until tender. Heat remaining oil in wok, add peas, stir-fry until just tender. Return chicken to wok with sauce, onion and radishes; cook, stirring, until hot.
3 Combine noodles and coriander in large bowl; serve topped with chicken mixture.

on the table in 30 minutes
serves 4
per serving 10.1g fat; 1835kJ (438 cal)

lemongrass chicken with vermicelli salad

250g bean thread vermicelli
1 tablespoon groundnut oil
600g chicken thigh fillets, sliced thinly
2 x 10cm sticks fresh lemongrass (20g), sliced thinly
1 clove garlic, crushed
1 tablespoon fish sauce
2 cups (120g) shredded iceberg lettuce
1 medium carrot (120g), cut into matchsticks
½ cucumber (130g), deseeded, sliced thinly
¼ cup (35g) coarsely chopped roasted unsalted peanuts
1 red radish (35g), trimmed, cut into thin strips

chilli dressing
¼ cup (75g) white sugar
½ cup (125ml) water
2 tablespoons white vinegar
1 fresh small red thai chilli, chopped finely

1 Place vermicelli in medium heatproof bowl, cover with boiling water; stand until just tender, drain.
2 Meanwhile, make chilli dressing.
3 Heat oil in wok; stir-fry chicken, in batches, until browned. Return chicken to wok with lemongrass and garlic; cook, stirring, until lemongrass softens. Add sauce; stir-fry until hot.
4 Serve vermicelli with lettuce, carrot, cucumber and chicken mixture, sprinkled with nuts, radish and half the dressing. Serve with remaining dressing.

chilli dressing Combine sugar and the water in small saucepan. Stir over low heat until sugar dissolves; bring to a boil. Reduce heat; simmer, uncovered, about 5 minutes or until mixture thickens slightly. Remove from heat; stir in vinegar and chilli.
on the table in 30 minutes
serves 4
per serving 20.4g fat; 2449kJ (586 cal)
tip You will need about a half a medium head of iceberg lettuce to get the amount required for this recipe.

thai chicken stir-fry

250g dried rice stick noodles
600g chicken thigh fillets, sliced thinly
⅓ cup (80ml) sweet chilli sauce
1 tablespoon groundnut oil
300g green beans, halved widthways
2 cloves garlic, crushed
2cm piece fresh ginger (10g), grated
2 fresh small red thai chillies, sliced thinly
2 tablespoons fish sauce
¼ cup (60ml) lime juice
6 spring onions, chopped coarsely
2 cups (160g) beansprouts
¼ cup firmly packed fresh coriander leaves
¼ cup firmly packed fresh mint leaves

1 Place noodles in large heatproof bowl, cover with boiling water; stand until just tender, drain.
2 Meanwhile, combine chicken and half the sweet chilli sauce in large bowl. Heat oil in wok; stir-fry chicken mixture, in batches.
3 Add beans, garlic, ginger and half the chilli to wok; stir-fry until beans are tender.
4 Return chicken to wok with noodles and remaining ingredients; stir-fry until hot. Serve with lime wedges, if desired.

on the table in 30 minutes
serves 4
per serving 17.1g fat; 2149kJ (514 cal)

stir-fried prawns & noodles

500g medium uncooked prawns
200g dried rice noodles
1 clove garlic, crushed
2 tablespoons soy sauce
2 tablespoons fish sauce
1 teaspoon sambal oelek
1 cup (80g) beansprouts
¼ cup fresh coriander leaves

1 Shell and devein prawns, leaving tails intact.
2 Place noodles in large heatproof bowl, cover with boiling water, stand until just tender; drain. Cover to keep warm.
3 Heat oiled wok or large pan; stir-fry prawns and garlic until prawns are just changed in colour. Add noodles, sauces and sambal; gently stir-fry until hot. Stir in beansprouts and coriander.

on the table in 30 minutes
serves 4
per serving 1g fat; 806kJ (193 cal)

teriyaki beef stir-fry

2 tablespoons groundnut oil
2 teaspoons sesame oil
2 cloves garlic, sliced thinly
600g piece rump steak, sliced thinly
1 medium brown onion (150g), sliced thickly
230g can bamboo shoots, drained
½ cup (40g) beansprouts
¼ cup (60ml) teriyaki sauce
⅓ cup (80ml) beef stock
450g hokkien noodles
4 spring onions, sliced thickly

1 Heat oils in wok or large non-stick frying pan; stir-fry garlic and beef, in batches, until beef is browned.
2 Stir-fry brown onion and bamboo shoots 2 minutes.
3 Return beef mixture to wok with beansprouts. Stir in sauce and stock; stir-fry until mixture boils.
4 Meanwhile, place noodles in medium heatproof bowl; cover with boiling water, separate with fork, drain. Serve stir-fry with the noodles; sprinkle with spring onions.

on the table in 35 minutes
serves 4
per serving 20g fat; 2643kJ (632 cal)
tip Recipe best made just before serving.

beef in black bean sauce with rice noodles & greens

250g dried rice stick noodles
1 tablespoon groundnut oil
600g minced beef
1 medium brown onion (150g), sliced thinly
2 fresh long red chillies, sliced thinly
350g chinese cabbage, chopped coarsely
150g sugar snap peas, trimmed
¼ cup (60ml) black bean sauce
¼ cup (60ml) kecap manis
1 tablespoon rice vinegar
¼ cup (80ml) beef stock
4 spring onions, sliced thinly

1 Place noodles in large heatproof bowl, cover with boiling water; stand until just tender, drain.
2 Meanwhile, heat oil in wok; stir-fry beef, onion and chilli until beef is cooked through.
3 Add chinese cabbage and peas; stir-fry until cabbage is tender.
4 Add noodles and combined remaining ingredients; stir-fry until hot.

on the table in 30 minutes
serves 4
per serving 16.5g fat; 2144kJ (513 cal)
tip You can buy jars of black bean and garlic sauce from supermarkets and Asian food shops.

stir-fried turkey with lemon & chilli

500g turkey breast fillets, sliced thinly
2 teaspoons finely grated lemon rind
2 birdseye chillies, deseeded, chopped finely
2 teaspoons olive oil
2 cloves garlic, crushed
1 tablespoon finely chopped fresh lemongrass
1 large (200g) brown onion, sliced thinly
600g fresh ramen noodles
300g baby pak choy, chopped
2 tablespoons black bean sauce
¼ cup (60ml) plum sauce
¾ cup (180ml) chicken stock

1 Combine turkey, rind and chilli in medium bowl. Heat 1 teaspoon of the oil in wok or large pan; stir-fry turkey mixture, in batches, until browned and tender.
2 Heat remaining oil in wok; stir-fry garlic, lemongrass and onion until onion is soft. Add noodles and pak choy; stir-fry until pak choy is just wilted. Return turkey to wok with sauces and stock; stir until sauce boils and thickens slightly.

on the table in 30 minutes
serves 4
per serving 9.1g fat; 3147kJ (752 cal)

satay pork & noodle stir-fry

500g fresh egg noodles
1 tablespoon vegetable oil
500g pork fillet, sliced thinly
2 cloves garlic, crushed
8 spring onions, sliced thinly
¾ cup (180ml) beef stock
⅓ cup (85g) crunchy peanut butter
¼ cup (60ml) sweet chilli sauce
2 teaspoons lemon juice
400g packet fresh Asian-style stir-fry vegetables

1 Place noodles in large heatproof bowl, cover with boiling water, stand until just tender; drain.
2 Heat half the oil in wok or large pan, stir-fry pork, in batches, until browned. Heat remaining oil in wok, add garlic and onion, stir-fry until soft.
3 Add stock, peanut butter, sauce and juice, simmer, uncovered, 1 minute. Return pork to wok with vegetables and noodles, cook, stirring, until hot.

on the table in 30 minutes
serves 4
per serving 12.7g fat; 1368kJ (327 cal)

pepperoni pizza

30cm homemade or purchased pizza base
⅓ cup (90g) tomato paste
2 teaspoons dried oregano
2 cups (200g) grated mozzarella cheese
¼ cup (20g) grated parmesan cheese
150g sliced pepperoni
½ cup (80g) pitted black olives

1 Place pizza base on oiled pizza tray. Spread base with combined tomato paste and oregano; sprinkle with two-thirds of the combined cheeses. Top with pepperoni and olives, then remaining cheeses.
2 Bake, uncovered, in moderately hot oven about 20 minutes or until base is cooked through and cheese is bubbling.

on the table in 30 minutes
serves 4
per serving 29g fat; 2311kJ (552 cal)
tip Any salami, cabanossi or ham can be substituted for the pepperoni.

tomato & onion pitta pizzas

4 wholemeal pitta
¼ cup (60ml) bottled tomato pasta sauce
1 cup (125g) grated cheddar cheese
2 medium tomatoes (380g), sliced thinly
1 medium brown onion (150g), sliced thinly
¼ cup (30g) pitted black olives, halved

1 Place pitta in single layer on lightly oiled oven tray. Spread each pitta with pasta sauce; top with half of the cheese. Top with tomato, onion and olives; sprinkle with remaining cheese.
2 Bake pizzas in hot oven about 15 minutes or until browned lightly.

on the table in 30 minutes
serves 4
per serving 16.7g fat; 1633kJ (390 cal)

pizza with prosciutto & ricotta

3 medium plum tomatoes (225g)
3 x 25cm homemade or purchased pizza bases
½ cup (140g) tomato paste
300g baby spinach
1 large red onion (300g), sliced thinly
9 slices prosciutto (135g), halved
¼ cup loosely packed, coarsely chopped fresh basil
1½ cups (300g) ricotta cheese
¼ cup (40g) pine nuts
¼ cup (60ml) olive oil
2 cloves garlic, crushed

1 Cut each tomato into eight wedges.
2 Place pizza bases on oven trays. Spread each base with a third of the tomato paste; top with equal amounts of tomato, spinach, onion, prosciutto, basil, cheese and pine nuts. Drizzle each pizza with equal amounts of combined oil and garlic.
3 Bake, uncovered, in very hot oven about 15 minutes or until pizza tops are browned lightly and bases are crisp.

on the table in 30 minutes
serves 6
per serving 27.6g fat; 2934kJ (701 cal)

salami, mushroom & oregano pizza

30cm homemade or purchased pizza base
¼ cup (70g) tomato paste
2 teaspoons dried oregano
⅓ cup (80ml) bottled tomato pasta sauce
½ cup (150g) coarsely chopped cooked swiss chard
50g button mushrooms, sliced thinly
100g sliced salami
¾ cup (75g) grated mozzarella cheese

1 Place pizza base on lightly oiled pizza tray. Spread combined tomato paste and oregano over pizza base. Top with pasta sauce, swiss chard, mushrooms, then salami. Sprinkle with cheese.
2 Bake, uncovered, in moderately hot oven, about 20 minutes or until base is cooked through and cheese is bubbling.

on the table in 35 minutes
serves 4
per serving 16.5g fat; 1596kJ (381 cal)
tips Split a purchased base in half for a thin crust pizza. Use cut-side up and bake about 5 minutes less than the time stated.
Use your choice of mild or hot salami for this pizza.

pesto, mozzarella & artichoke pizza

30cm homemade or purchased pizza base
190g jar pesto
100g marinated aubergine slices
200g char-grilled pepper slices
2 drained marinated artichoke hearts, sliced thickly
200g mozzarella, sliced thickly
2 tablespoons pine nuts

1 Place pizza base on oiled pizza tray. Spread pesto over base; top with aubergine, pepper and artichokes. Arrange mozzarella on top; sprinkle with pine nuts.
2 Bake, uncovered, in moderately hot oven about 20 minutes or until base is cooked through and cheese is bubbling.

on the table in 35 minutes
serves 4
per serving 40.1g fat; 2581kJ (616 cal)
tip The same amount of ingredients used to top a 30cm pizza will top four mini pizza bases.

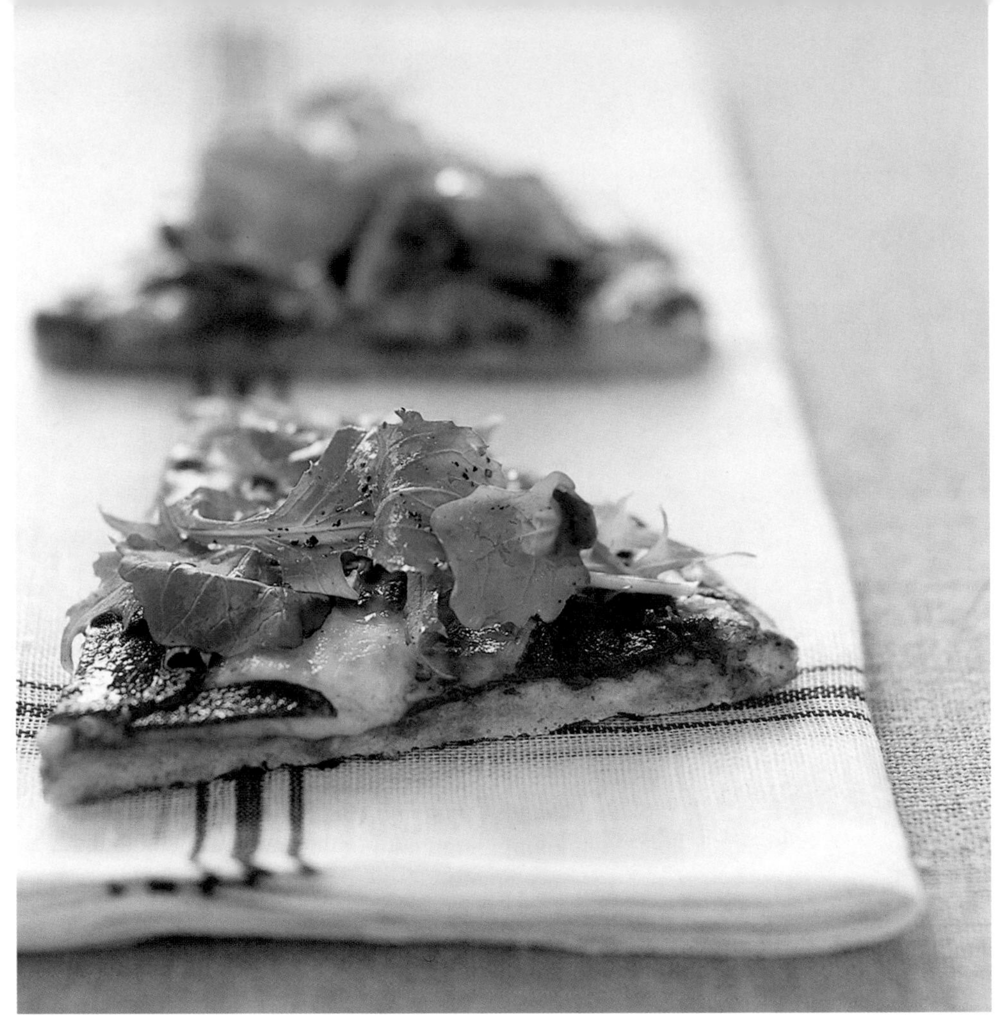

salami & rocket pizza

2 x 26cm pizza bases
⅔ cup (160ml) tomato pasta sauce
250g mozzarella cheese, sliced thinly
125g salami, sliced thinly
50g baby rocket leaves

1 Preheat oven to hot.
2 Place pizza bases on oven trays. Spread sauce evenly over bases; top with cheese and salami. Bake, uncovered, in hot oven about 15 minutes or until cheese melts and bases are crisp.
3 Just before serving, top pizzas with rocket and freshly ground pepper, if desired.

on the table in 25 minutes
serves 4
per serving 30.3g fat; 2818kJ (673 cal)
tips Pizza is best made just before serving.
Any fresh or frozen pizza bases would be suitable.

mushroom pizza

4 x 15cm pizza bases
1½ cups (185g) grated pizza cheese
150g flat mushrooms, sliced thinly
100g feta cheese, crumbled
2 tablespoons finely chopped fresh chives

1 Preheat oven to hot. Place pizza bases on oven tray. Sprinkle half the pizza cheese over bases. Divide mushroom, feta cheese, chives and remaining pizza cheese among bases.
2 Bake, uncovered, in hot oven about 15 minutes or until pizza tops are browned lightly and bases are crisp.

on the table in 25 minutes
serves 4
per serving 22.1g fat; 2325kJ (556 cal)
tips We used a Greek feta, which crumbles well and has a sharp taste, for this recipe.
Any fresh or frozen pizza bases would be suitable.

pasta

scallops with asparagus

- 375g large pasta spirals
- 2 teaspoons olive oil
- 500g asparagus, trimmed, cut into 5cm lengths
- 400g scallops
- 1 cup (250ml) dry white wine
- 300ml cream
- 2 tablespoons fresh dill tips
- 1 tablespoon finely shredded lemon rind
- 1 tablespoon lemon juice

1 Cook pasta in large saucepan of boiling water, uncovered, until just tender; drain.

2 While pasta is cooking, heat half of the oil in large frying pan; cook asparagus, in batches, stirring, until just tender.

3 Heat remaining oil in same pan; cook scallops, in batches, until browned both sides. Add wine to same pan; boil, uncovered, until reduced by three-quarters. Reduce heat, add cream; simmer, uncovered, until sauce thickens slightly.

4 Place pasta in pan with asparagus, scallops and remaining ingredients; toss gently over low heat until hot.

on the table in 25 minutes
serves 4
per serving 36.9g fat; 3139kJ (750 cal)

fresh tomato & caper salsa with penne

375g penne
6 medium tomatoes (1.1kg), deseeded, chopped finely
⅓ cup (80g) drained capers, chopped coarsely
1 medium red onion (170g), chopped finely
12 basil leaves, torn
12 purple basil leaves, torn
½ cup (80g) toasted pine nuts

balsamic vinaigrette
2 cloves garlic, crushed
⅓ cup (80ml) balsamic vinegar
⅔ cup (160ml) olive oil

1 Cook pasta in large saucepan of boiling water, uncovered, until tender; drain. Rinse until cold water; drain.
2 Place pasta in large bowl with remaining ingredients; drizzle with balsamic vinaigrette, toss gently to combine.

balsamic vinaigrette Combine garlic, vinegar and oil in screw-top jar; shake well.
on the table in 25 minutes
serves 4
per serving 51.7g fat; 2297kJ (549 cal)

spaghetti with baked ricotta

2 x 270g jars marinated aubergine in oil
2 cloves garlic, crushed
375g spaghetti
2 x 415g cans tomatoes
½ teaspoon cracked black pepper
300g baked ricotta, chopped coarsely

1 Cook undrained aubergine and garlic in large saucepan, stirring, until fragrant. Meanwhile, cook pasta in large saucepan of boiling water, uncovered, until just tender; drain.
2 Stir pasta, undrained crushed tomatoes and pepper into aubergine mixture; toss over medium heat until combined, then gently stir in ricotta.
on the table in 20 minutes
serves 4
per serving 32.4g fat; 3352kJ (801 cal)
tip You can use any kind of marinated vegetables (mushrooms, peppers or mixed antipasti) in this recipe instead of the aubergine.

macaroni cheese

250g macaroni
60g butter
⅓ cup (50g) plain flour
3 cups (750ml) milk
2 cups (250g) coarsely grated pizza cheese

1 Cook pasta in large saucepan of boiling water, uncovered, until just tender; drain. While pasta is cooking, melt butter in medium saucepan, add flour; cook, stirring, about 2 minutes or until mixture thickens and bubbles. Gradually stir in milk; cook, stirring, until sauce boils and thickens.
2 Stir pasta and half of the cheese into sauce; pour mixture into shallow 2-litre (8-cup) baking dish. Sprinkle with remaining cheese; place under hot grill until cheese melts and is browned lightly.

on the table in 25 minutes
serves 4
per serving 34.2g fat; 2846kJ (680 cal)
tip This quick version doesn't have to go into the oven, like the traditional macaroni cheese recipe, so it's great when you want dinner on the table fast.

fettuccine carbonara

4 (280g) bacon rashers, chopped coarsely
375g fettuccine
3 egg yolks, beaten lightly
1 cup (250ml) cream
½ cup (30g) finely grated parmesan
2 tablespoons coarsely chopped fresh chives

1 Cook bacon in heated small frying pan, stirring, until crisp; drain.
2 Just before serving, cook pasta in large saucepan of boiling water, uncovered, until just tender; drain.
3 Combine pasta in large bowl with egg yolks, cream and cheese; sprinkle with chives.

on the table in 20 minutes
serves 4
per serving 34.2g fat; 2762kJ (660 cal)
tips Try using grated romano or pepato cheese instead of parmesan.
You can use pancetta or prosciutto instead of the bacon if you prefer.

fettuccine alfredo

375g fettuccine
2 teaspoons olive oil
4 spring onions, sliced thinly
1 clove garlic, crushed
2 tablespoons dry white wine
300ml cream
1 teaspoon dijon mustard
¼ cup loosely packed, finely chopped fresh flat-leaf parsley
1 cup (80g) finely grated parmesan

1 Cook pasta in large saucepan of boiling water, uncovered, until just tender; drain.
2 While pasta is cooking, heat oil in medium saucepan; cook onion and garlic, stirring, until onion softens. Add wine and cream; bring to a boil. Reduce heat; simmer, stirring, about 2 minutes or until sauce is smooth. Stir in mustard.
3 Add pasta, parsley and cheese to sauce; toss gently to combine.
on the table in 30 minutes
serves 4
per serving 43g fat; 3148kJ (752 cal)

roasted sweet potato & parmesan pasta

1 large sweet potato (500g)
2 tablespoons olive oil
250g curly lasagne
1 cup (80g) shaved parmesan
250g rocket leaves, torn
¼ cup (60ml) balsamic vinegar
¼ cup (60ml) olive oil, extra
1 clove garlic, crushed

1 Preheat oven to very hot. Halve sweet potato lengthways; slice halves into 5mm pieces. Combine sweet potato with oil in large baking dish; roast, uncovered, in very hot oven about 25 minutes or until tender.
2 Meanwhile, break lasagne roughly lengthways, cook in large saucepan of boiling water, uncovered, until just tender; drain.
3 Place pasta, sweet potato, cheese, rocket and combined remaining ingredients in large bowl; toss gently to combine.
on the table in 35 minutes
serves 4
per serving 30.5g fat; 2500kJ (597 cal)
tip In this recipe we used broken curly lasagne, sometimes called pappardelle or lasagnette, for the casual look we wanted with the sweet potato. You can substitute any shape pasta you prefer.

gnocchi al quattro formaggi

¼ cup (60ml) dry white wine
1 cup (250g) mascarpone cheese
1 cup (120g) coarsely grated mozzarella
½ cup (40g) coarsely grated parmesan
¼ cup (60ml) milk
625g gnocchi
75g gorgonzola cheese, crumbled

1 Add wine to large saucepan; boil, uncovered, until wine reduces by half. Reduce heat, add mascarpone; stir until mixture is smooth. Add mozzarella, parmesan and milk; cook, stirring, until cheeses melt and sauce is smooth in consistency.
2 Meanwhile, cook gnocchi in large saucepan of boiling water, uncovered, until gnocchi rise to the surface and are just tender; drain.
3 Add gnocchi and gorgonzola to sauce; toss gently to combine.

on the table in 20 minutes
serves 4
per serving 52.3g fat; 3068kJ (733 cal)
tip If this pasta dish, with its sauce of four cheeses, is served as a first course, try not to follow it with a main course that's equally rich. Grilled plain chops or poached fish fillets are perfect possibilities.

spaghetti with chilli & leek

4 (280g) rashers bacon, chopped coarsely
375g spaghetti
80g butter
2 small leeks (400g), sliced thinly
2 cloves garlic, crushed
2 red thai chillies, chopped finely
6 spring onions, chopped finely
½ cup (40g) finely grated parmesan

1 Cook bacon in large heated dry frying pan, stirring, until browned; drain on absorbent paper.
2 Cook pasta in large saucepan of boiling water, uncovered, until just tender; drain.
3 While pasta is cooking, melt butter in medium frying pan; cook leek and garlic, stirring, about 5 minutes or until leek softens. Add bacon, chilli and onion; cook, stirring, 2 minutes or until onion softens.
4 Place pasta in large bowl with leek mixture and cheese; toss gently to combine.

on the table in 25 minutes
serves 4
per serving 24.2g fat; 2441kJ (583 cal)
tip For a milder version, remove seeds from the chillies.

fettuccine alle vongole

2 tablespoons olive oil
3 cloves garlic, crushed
1 fresh long red chilli, chopped finely
1 tablespoon drained baby capers, rinsed
¾ cup (180ml) dry white wine
¾ cup (180ml) fish stock
2 tablespoons lemon juice
1kg clams
375g fettuccine
½ cup coarsely chopped fresh flat-leaf parsley
¼ cup coarsely chopped fresh chives

1 Heat oil in large saucepan; cook garlic and chilli, stirring, 1 minute. Add capers, wine, stock and juice; bring to a boil. Add clams; cook vongole mixture, covered, about 5 minutes or until clams open (discard any that do not).
2 Meanwhile, cook pasta in large saucepan of boiling water, uncovered, until just tender; drain.
3 Add pasta with herbs to vongole mixture; toss gently to combine.

on the table in 30 minutes
serves 4
per serving 11.3g fat; 2068kJ (494 cal)
tip A classic pasta vongole is made with tiny baby clams in Italy, but you can use a mixture of any available bivalves for this recipe.

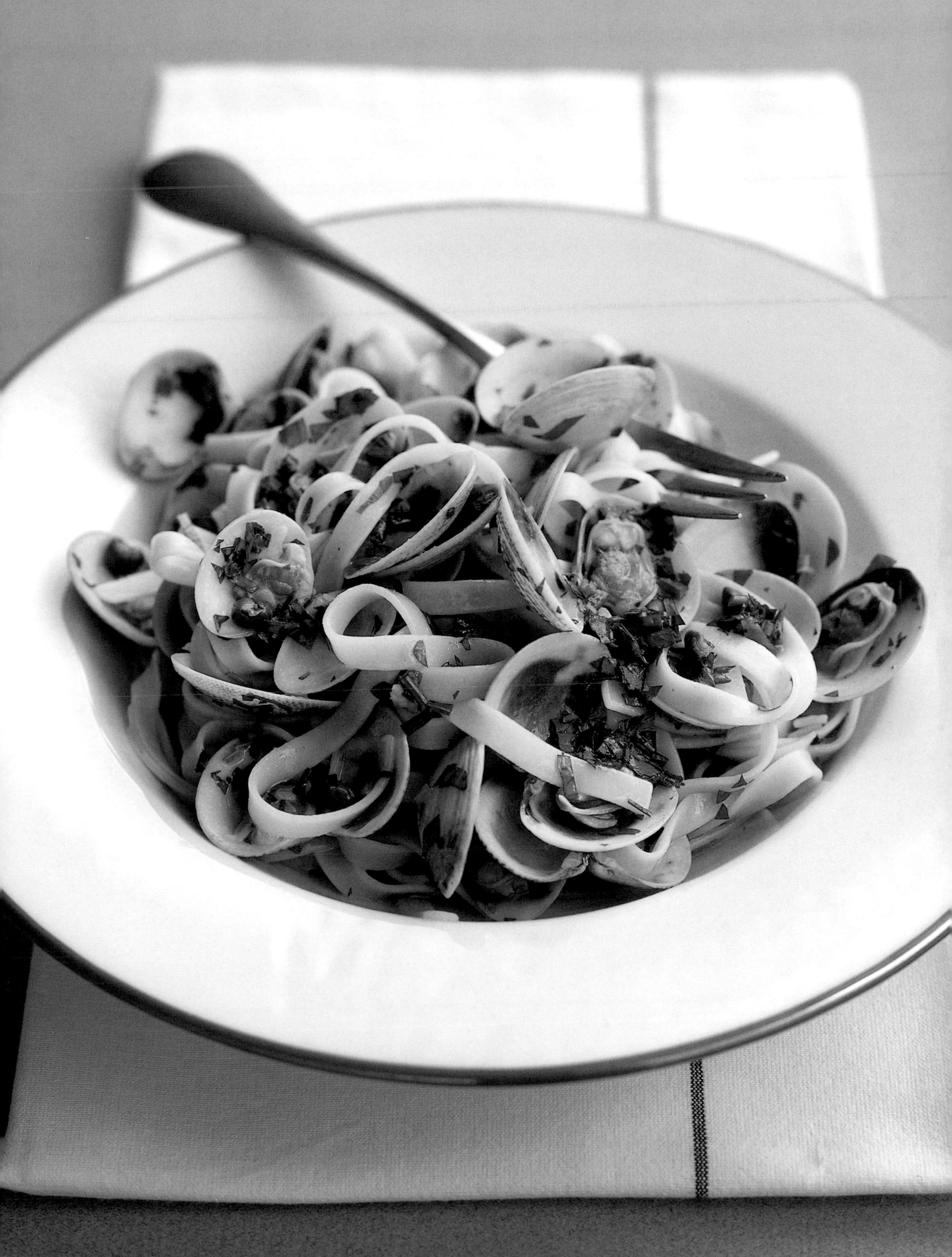

roasted pepper, goat's cheese & walnut salad

375g large pasta spirals
2 medium red peppers (400g)
2 medium yellow peppers (400g)
150g goat's cheese, crumbled
⅓ cup (35g) walnuts, toasted, chopped coarsely
½ cup loosely packed fresh basil leaves
¼ cup (60ml) red wine vinegar
⅓ cup (80ml) olive oil
1 clove garlic, crushed
2 teaspoons wholegrain mustard

1 Cook pasta in large saucepan of boiling water, uncovered, until just tender; drain. Rinse under cold water; drain.
2 Meanwhile, quarter peppers, remove and discard seeds and membranes. Roast under grill or in very hot oven, skin-side up, until skin blisters and blackens. Cover pepper pieces with plastic or paper for 5 minutes, peel away skin; slice pepper thickly.
3 Place pasta and pepper in large bowl with cheese, walnuts, basil and combined remaining ingredients; toss gently to combine.

on the table in 30 minutes
serves 4
per serving 31.5g fat; 2703kJ (646 cal)
tip Feta or any soft, crumbly cheese can be used instead of the goat's cheese, and toasted pecan halves make a nice change from walnuts.

fettuccine with rocket pesto & fresh tomato salsa

500g fettuccine pasta
8 cloves garlic, quartered
½ cup coarsely chopped fresh basil
120g rocket, chopped coarsely
⅔ cup (160ml) olive oil
½ cup (40g) finely grated parmesan cheese
3 medium tomatoes (570g), chopped coarsely
2 tablespoons lemon juice
2 fresh small red thai chillies, sliced thinly
⅓ cup (50g) pine nuts, toasted

1 Cook pasta in large saucepan of boiling water, uncovered, until just tender; drain.
2 Meanwhile, blend or process garlic, basil, rocket and oil until smooth.
3 Combine pasta, rocket pesto, cheese, tomato, juice and chilli in large saucepan; cook, stirring, until hot. Add nuts; toss gently to combine.

on the table in 25 minutes
serves 4
per serving 50.3g fat; 3780kJ (904 cal)
tip You can substitute baby spinach leaves for the rocket for a milder pesto.

pasta with peas & prosciutto

1 tablespoon olive oil
1 large brown onion (200g), sliced thickly
1 clove garlic, crushed
6 slices prosciutto (100g), chopped coarsely
600ml bottled tomato pasta sauce
½ cup (125ml) cream
2 cups (250g) frozen peas
250g curly lasagne

1 Heat oil in large saucepan; cook onion, garlic and prosciutto, stirring, until onion softens. Add sauce, cream and peas; bring to a boil. Reduce heat; simmer, uncovered, until sauce thickens slightly.
2 Meanwhile, cook pasta in large saucepan of boiling water, uncovered, until just tender; drain.
3 Place pasta in large bowl with sauce; toss gently to combine.

on the table in 20 minutes
serves 4
per serving 20.8g fat; 2163kJ (517 cal)

mixed-mushroom orecchiette

1 tablespoon olive oil
1 medium brown onion (150g), chopped finely
2 cloves garlic, crushed
250g button mushrooms, sliced thickly
250g chestnut mushrooms, sliced thickly
250g flat mushrooms, sliced thickly
250g spreadable cream cheese
½ cup (125ml) chicken stock
375g orecchiette pasta
½ teaspoon cracked black pepper
2 tablespoons coarsely chopped fresh flat-leaf parsley

1 Heat oil in large frying pan; cook onion and garlic, stirring, until onion softens. Add mushrooms; cook, stirring, until browned and tender. Add cream cheese and stock; cook over low heat, stirring, until cheese melts and mixture is hot.
2 Meanwhile, cook pasta in large saucepan of boiling water, uncovered, until just tender; drain. Place pasta in pan with mushroom sauce; stir in pepper and parsley, toss gently to combine.

on the table in 25 minutes
serves 4
per serving 26.9g fat; 2615kJ (625 cal)

risoni with spinach & semi-dried tomatoes

30g butter
2 medium brown onions (300g), chopped finely
3 cloves garlic, crushed
500g risoni pasta
4 cups (1 litre) chicken stock
½ cup (125ml) dry white wine
150g semi-dried tomatoes, halved
100g baby spinach leaves
⅓ cup (25g) finely grated parmesan

1 Melt butter in large saucepan; cook onion and garlic, stirring, until onion softens. Add risoni; stir to coat in butter mixture. Stir in stock and wine; bring to a boil.
2 Reduce heat; simmer over medium heat, stirring, until liquid is absorbed and risoni is just tender. Gently stir in tomato, spinach and cheese.

on the table in 30 minutes
serves 4
per serving 12.5g fat; 2777kJ (663 cal)
tip Risoni is a small pasta shaped like a grain of rice. You can substiture any small pasta in this recipe.

tagliatelle puttanesca

2 teaspoons vegetable oil
1 large brown onion (200g), sliced thickly
3 cloves garlic, crushed
4 red thai chillies, deseeded, chopped finely
600ml bottled tomato pasta sauce
¼ cup (40g) drained capers
1 cup (160g) kalamata olives, pitted
8 drained anchovies, halved
½ cup coarsely chopped fresh flat-leaf parsley
375g tagliatelle

1 Heat oil in large frying pan; cook onion, garlic and chilli, stirring, until onion softens. Add sauce, capers, olives and anchovies; bring to a boil. Reduce heat; simmer, uncovered, about 5 minutes or until sauce thickens slightly. Stir in parsley.
2 Cook pasta in large saucepan of boiling water, uncovered, until just tender; drain. Serve pasta with sauce.

on the table in 30 minutes
serves 4
per serving 4.7g fat; 1902kJ (454 cal)

aubergine pasta sauce

¼ cup (60ml) olive oil
1 medium brown onion (150g), chopped finely
2 trimmed celery sticks (150g), chopped finely
1 clove garlic, crushed
2 tablespoons brandy
1 medium aubergine (300g), sliced thinly
600ml bottled tomato pasta sauce
½ cup (140g) tomato paste
½ cup (125ml) water
375g rigatoni pasta
¼ cup (20g) finely grated parmesan

1 Heat oil in large saucepan; cook onion, celery and garlic, stirring, until onion softens. Add brandy; cook, stirring, until brandy evaporates. Add aubergine; cook, stirring, until aubergine is tender.
2 Stir in sauce, paste and the water; bring to a boil. Reduce heat; simmer, uncovered, about 10 minutes or until sauce thickens slightly.
3 Meanwhile, cook pasta in large saucepan of boiling water, uncovered, until just tender; drain. Place pasta in large bowl with half of the aubergine sauce; toss gently to combine. Divide pasta among serving plates; top each with remaining sauce and cheese.

on the table in 30 minutes
serves 4
per serving 16.9g fat; 2420kJ (578 cal)

orecchiette with artichokes, ham & sun-dried tomatoes

375g orecchiette
340g jar artichoke hearts in oil, drained, quartered
500g ham, sliced thickly
½ cup (75g) sun-dried tomatoes, halved
1 cup (80g) flaked parmesan
1 cup loosely packed fresh flat-leaf parsley
2 tablespoons lemon juice
1 tablespoon wholegrain mustard
1 tablespoon honey
1 clove garlic, crushed
½ cup (125ml) olive oil

1 Cook pasta in large saucepan of boiling water, uncovered, until just tender; drain.
2 Place pasta in large bowl with artichokes, ham, tomato, cheese, parsley and combined remaining ingredients; toss gently to combine.

on the table in 25 minutes
serves 4
per serving 46.1g fat; 3771kJ (901 cal)
tip If you can find fresh orecchiette (little ears), use them instead of the packaged dried version.

greek lamb, feta & aubergine pasta

1 medium aubergine (300g), chopped coarsely
cooking salt
500g lamb fillets
2 tablespoons olive oil
250g large pasta shells
1 medium red onion (170g), sliced
100g baby rocket leaves
2 medium tomatoes (380g), deseeded, sliced thinly
¼ cup loosely packed fresh oregano leaves
200g feta cheese, crumbled

balsamic vinaigrette
¼ cup (60ml) balsamic vinegar
½ cup (125ml) olive oil
2 cloves garlic, crushed
2 tablespoons wholegrain mustard

1 Place aubergine in colander, sprinkle all over with salt. Stand 5 minutes; rinse under cold water, drain on absorbent paper.
2 Meanwhile, cook lamb, in batches, in large non-stick frying pan until browned and cooked as desired. Stand 5 minutes; cut into thick slices.
3 Heat oil in same pan; cook aubergine, in batches, until browned all over and tender.
4 Meanwhile, cook pasta in large saucepan of boiling water, uncovered, until just tender; drain. Place pasta, lamb and aubergine in large bowl with remaining ingredients; drizzle with dressing, toss gently to combine.

balsamic vinaigrette Combine ingredients in screw-top jar; shake well.
on the table in 35 minutes
serves 4
per serving 55.1g fat; 3636kJ (868 cal)

chicken & fennel spirals

2 medium fennel bulbs (1kg), trimmed, sliced thinly
3 cloves garlic, sliced thinly
¼ cup (60ml) dry sherry
1½ cups (375ml) chicken stock
375g large pasta spirals
2 cups (340g) shredded cooked chicken
200g mangetout, trimmed, sliced thinly
1 cup (240g) soured cream
1 tablespoon coarsely chopped fresh tarragon

1 Preheat oven to very hot.
2 Combine fennel, garlic, sherry and ½ cup of the stock in large baking dish; roast, uncovered, in very hot oven about 15 minutes or until fennel is just tender.
3 Cook pasta in large saucepan of boiling water, uncovered, until just tender; drain.
4 Place fennel mixture and pasta in same cleaned pan with remaining ingredients; stir over low heat until hot.

on the table in 30 minutes
serves 4
per serving 31.5g fat; 3106kJ (742 cal)

chicken liver sauce with curly lasagne

500g chicken livers
½ cup (50g) packaged breadcrumbs
¼ cup (60ml) olive oil
1 medium brown onion (150g), chopped coarsely
4 medium tomatoes (520g), chopped coarsely
½ cup (125ml) chicken stock
¼ cup (60ml) balsamic vinegar
¼ cup (60ml) dry red wine
2 tablespoons coarsely chopped fresh rosemary
375g curly lasagne

1 Halve each trimmed chicken liver lobe; toss in breadcrumbs, shaking off excess. Heat half of the oil in large frying pan; cook liver over high heat, in batches, until browned and cooked as desired.
2 Heat remaining oil in same pan; cook onion, stirring, until soft. Add tomato; cook, stirring, until tomato is pulpy. Add stock, vinegar, wine and rosemary to pan; cook, stirring, until sauce thickens slightly.
3 Meanwhile, cook pasta in large saucepan of boiling water, uncovered, until just tender; drain. Stir pasta and liver into tomato sauce; toss gently to combine.

on the table in 30 minutes
serves 4
per serving 20.3g fat; 2765kJ (660 cal)
tip Be sure not to overcook the chicken livers or they will be dry and unappealing.

fish & seafood

moroccan fish fillets with fruity couscous

1 clove garlic, crushed
1cm piece fresh ginger (5g), grated finely
1 teaspoon ground cumin
½ teaspoon ground turmeric
½ teaspoon hot paprika
½ teaspoon ground coriander
4 x 200g white fish fillets, skinned
1 tablespoon olive oil

fruity couscous
2 cups (400g) couscous
2 cups (500ml) boiling water
50g butter
1 large pear (330g), chopped finely
½ cup (75g) finely chopped dried apricots
½ cup (95g) coarsely chopped dried figs
½ cup coarsely chopped fresh flat-leaf parsley
¼ cup (40g) toasted pine nuts

1 Combine garlic, ginger and spices in large bowl. Add fish; toss to coat fish in spice mixture. Heat oil in large frying pan; cook fish, in batches, until browned both sides and cooked as desired.
2 Meanwhile, make fruity couscous.
3 Divide couscous among serving plates; top with fish. Accompany with a bowl of combined yogurt and coarsely chopped fresh coriander, if desired.

fruity couscous Combine couscous, the water and butter in large heatproof bowl, cover; stand about 5 minutes or until water is absorbed, fluffing with fork occasionally. Stir in remaining ingredients.

on the table in 35 minutes
serves 4
per serving 27.5g fat; 3816kJ (912 cal)

fish milanese

- 1 small brown onion (80g), chopped finely
- 2 tablespoons lemon juice
- ⅓ cup (80ml) olive oil
- 4 white fish fillets
- plain flour
- 2 eggs, beaten lightly
- 1 tablespoon milk
- 1 cup (100g) packaged breadcrumbs
- 1 tablespoon olive oil, extra
- 120g butter
- 1 clove garlic, crushed
- 2 teaspoons finely chopped fresh parsley

1 Combine onion, juice and oil in medium shallow bowl; mix well. Add fish; spoon mixture over fish to coat thoroughly. Cover; refrigerate 1 hour, turning occasionally.

2 Remove fish from marinade. Coat lightly with flour; shake away excess. Combine egg and milk in small bowl; dip fish into egg mixture. Coat in breadcrumbs; press on firmly.

3 Heat extra oil and half of the butter in large frying pan. Cook fish about 3 minutes each side, or until cooked through; drain on absorbent paper.

4 Heat remaining butter in small saucepan. Cook garlic until butter turns light golden brown; add parsley. Pour browned butter over fish.

on the table in 30 minutes
serves 4
per serving 52.4g fat; 2602kJ (621 cal)

calamari

- 1 egg
- 2 tablespoons milk
- 1kg calamari rings, sliced thinly
- 2 cups (200g) packaged breadcrumbs
- vegetable oil for deep-frying

1 Beat egg and milk in small bowl. Dip calamari in egg mixture; drain away excess. Toss in breadcrumbs; press breadcrumbs on firmly.

2 Heat oil in large saucepan. Deep-fry calamari, in batches, about 2 minutes or until golden brown; drain on absorbent paper. Serve with lemon wedges and tartare sauce, if desired.

on the table in 30 minutes
serves 4
per serving 19.2g fat; 1474kJ (352 cal)
tips Two cloves of crushed garlic can be added to the egg mixture.
Calamari can be shallow-fried. Heat a small amount of oil in large frying pan; the oil should reach only halfway up the side of each calamari ring. Cook calamari rings in hot oil, about 2 minutes each side, or until golden brown.

grilled snapper fillets with fennel & onion salad

1 medium red onion (170g), sliced thinly
4 spring onions, sliced thinly
1 large fennel bulb (550g), trimmed, sliced thinly
2 trimmed celery stalks (150g), sliced thinly
½ cup coarsely chopped fresh flat-leaf parsley
⅓ cup (80ml) orange juice
¼ cup (60ml) olive oil
2 cloves garlic, crushed
2 teaspoons sambal oelek
4 x 275g snapper fillets, with skin

1 Combine onions, fennel, celery and parsley in medium bowl.
2 Place juice, oil, garlic and sambal in screw-top jar; shake well.
3 Cook fish on heated oiled grill plate (or grill or barbecue) until browned both sides and cooked as desired.
4 Pour half of the dressing over salad in bowl; toss gently to combine. Serve salad topped with fish; drizzle with remaining dressing.

on the table in 25 minutes
serves 4
per serving 18.9g fat; 1813kJ (433 cal)

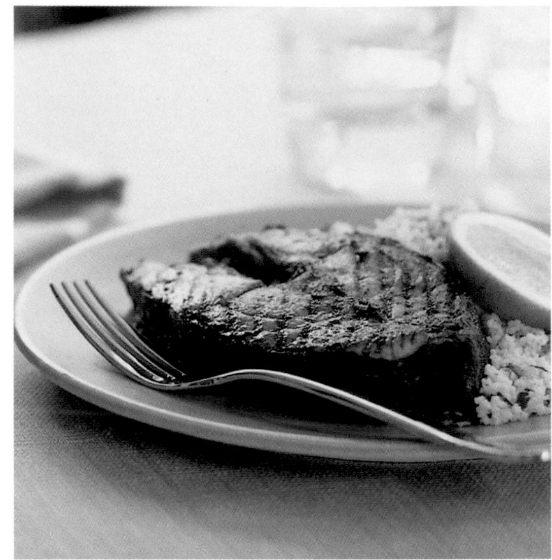

sardines with tomatoes & caper dressing

16 fresh sardines (750g), cleaned
4 medium plum tomatoes (300g), sliced thickly
1 small red onion (100g), sliced thinly
1 tablespoon coarsely chopped fresh flat-leaf parsley

caper dressing
⅓ cup (80ml) red wine vinegar
¼ cup (60ml) extra virgin olive oil
1 tablespoon drained baby capers
1 clove garlic, crushed
1 tablespoon finely chopped fresh parsley

1 To butterfly the sardines, cut through the underside to the tail. Break backbone at tail; peel away backbone. Trim sardines.
2 Cook sardines on heated, oiled grill plate (or grill or barbecue), in batches, until browned both sides and just cooked through. Serve with tomato and onion. Spoon over caper dressing; top with parsley.

caper dressing Combine ingredients in screw-top jar; shake well.
on the table in 30 minutes
serves 4
per serving 33.9g fat; 2039kJ (487 cal)
tip Have sardines cleaned and the heads removed at the fishmonger; they may even butterfly them for you.

fish cutlets in hot & spicy marinade

4 white fish cutlets (1kg)

marinade
1 tablespoon paprika
2 teaspoons ground ginger
1 teaspoon curry powder
¼ teaspoon chilli powder
¼ cup (60ml) brown vinegar
¼ cup (60ml) tomato paste
1 cup (250ml) dry white wine
2 cloves garlic, crushed

1 Combine fish and marinade in large bowl. Cover; refrigerate 3 hours or overnight.
2 Remove fish from marinade; discard marinade.
3 Cook fish on heated oiled grill plate (or grill or barbecue) until cooked as desired; remove from pan. Serve with couscous and lemon, if desired.

marinade Combine ingredients in medium bowl; mix well.
on the table in 20 minutes
serves 4
per serving 5g fat; 1134kJ (271 cal)
tip Fish is best marinated a day ahead and refrigerated, covered; uncooked marinated fish is suitable to freeze.

pan-fried fish steaks with rosemary & oregano

4 firm white fish steaks (800g)
¼ cup (60ml) lemon juice
½ cup (125ml) extra virgin olive oil
1 teaspoon salt
2 teaspoons finely chopped fresh oregano
2 teaspoons finely chopped fresh rosemary

1 Cook fish on heated oiled grill plate (or grill or barbecue) until cooked through; turn once during cooking.
2 Meanwhile, combine remaining ingredients in screw-top jar; shake well.
3 Brush both sides of hot fish with herb dressing; serve with any remaining dressing and patty-pan squash, if desired.

on the table in 12 minutes
serves 4
per serving 32.9g fat; 1924kJ (460 cal)
tip Any firm white fish cutlets are suitable for this recipe.

fish with garlic & chilli

¼ cup (60ml) olive oil
4 blue eye fish fillets with skin on (800g)
1 clove garlic, crushed
1½ tablespoons sherry vinegar
1 teaspoon dried chilli flakes
2 tablespoons chopped fresh flat-leaf parsley

1 Heat 1 tablespoon of the oil in large non-stick frying pan. Cook fish, flesh-side down, until well browned. Turn fish; cook until browned and just cooked through.
2 Meanwhile, place remaining oil, garlic, vinegar, chilli and parsley in small saucepan; stir over low heat until just warm – do not overheat. Spoon oil mixture over fish. Serve with lemon wedges and steamed zucchini and beans, if desired.

on the table in 13 minutes
serves 4
per serving 18.2g fat; 1376kJ (329 cal)
tip Sherry vinegar is available in some supermarkets; if unavailable, substitute red or white wine vinegar.

steamed scallops with asian flavours

1½ cups (300g) jasmine rice
3cm piece fresh ginger (15g)
20 scallops (800g), in half shell, roe removed
2 tablespoons thinly sliced fresh lemongrass
4 spring onions, sliced thinly
1 tablespoon sesame oil
¼ cup (60ml) kecap manis
¼ cup (60ml) soy sauce

1 Cook rice in large saucepan of boiling water, uncovered, until just tender; drain.
2 Meanwhile, slice ginger thinly; cut slices into thin strips. Place scallops, in batches, in single layer in large bamboo steamer; top with ginger, lemongrass and onion. Cover then steam scallops about 5 minutes or until tender and cooked as desired.
3 Divide scallops among serving plates; top scallops with combined remaining ingredients. Serve with rice.

on the table in 30 minutes
serves 4
per serving 5.6g fat; 1509kJ (361 cal)
tip You can also use scallops with the roe attached, if you prefer.

smoked trout & crisp noodle salad

450g smoked ocean trout fillets
3½ cups (280g) finely shredded red cabbage
2 medium carrots (240g), grated coarsely
2 x 100g packets fried noodles
4 spring onions, sliced thinly
2 tablespoons toasted sesame seeds
½ cup (125ml) sweet chilli sauce
1 tablespoon sesame oil
2 tablespoons white wine vinegar
2 tablespoons soy sauce

1 Discard any skin and bones from fish. Flake fish in large bowl; add cabbage, carrot, noodles, onion and seeds.
2 Place remaining ingredients in screw-top jar; shake well. Drizzle dressing over salad; toss gently to combine.

on the table in 25 minutes
serves 4
per serving 19.4g fat; 1701kJ (406 cal)
tips Filleted portions of smoked trout, in a variety of sizes, are now available at most supermarkets; we used three 150g portions for this recipe.
Fried noodles are crisp wheat noodles packaged (commonly in 100g packets) already deep-fried.
You need a quarter of a medium red cabbage, about 375g, for this recipe.

crab & apple salad

250g sugar snap peas, trimmed
1 large apple (200g)
500g cooked crab meat
1 medium red onion (170g), halved, sliced thinly
2 fresh red thai chillies, deseeded, sliced thinly lengthways
2 medium avocados (500g), sliced thickly
150g mixed salad leaves
⅓ cup (80ml) olive oil
¼ cup (60ml) lemon juice
1 tablespoon dijon mustard
1 clove garlic, crushed

1 Boil, steam or microwave peas until just tender; drain. Rinse under cold water; drain.
2 Slice apple thinly; cut slices into thin strips. Combine peas and apple in large bowl with crab, onion, chilli, avocado and salad leaves.
3 Place remaining ingredients in screw-top jar; shake well. Drizzle dressing over salad; toss gently to combine.

on the table in 25 minutes
serves 4
per serving 40.1g fat; 2094kJ (500 cal)

chicken

chicken caesar salad

4 slices white bread (180g)
2 tablespoons olive oil
4 bacon rashers (280g), rind removed, sliced thinly
3 cups (480g) coarsely chopped barbecued chicken
1 large cos lettuce, trimmed and torn
6 spring onions, sliced thinly
1 cup (80g) flaked parmesan

caesar dressing

¾ cup (225g) whole-egg mayonnaise
1 tablespoon lemon juice
4 drained anchovy fillets, chopped finely
3 teaspoons dijon mustard
1 tablespoon water

1 Preheat oven to moderate.
2 Make caesar dressing by blending or processing ingredients until mixture is smooth.
3 Remove crusts from bread; discard crusts, cut bread into 2cm squares; toss with oil in medium bowl. Place bread, in single layer, on oven tray; toast in oven, 10 minutes.
4 Cook bacon in small frying pan, stirring, until browned and crisp. Drain on absorbent paper.
5 Combine half of the chicken, half of the bacon, half of the croutons and half of the dressing in large bowl with lettuce, half of the onion and half of the cheese; toss to combine.
6 Divide salad among serving plates. Top with remaining chicken, bacon, croutons, onion and cheese; drizzle with remaining dressing.

caesar dressing Blend or process all ingredients together until mixture is smooth.
on the table in 25 minutes
serves 4
per serving 49.9g fat; 3390kJ (811 cal)

tandoori chicken

½ cup (140g) low-fat plain yogurt
1 tablespoon lemon juice
½ teaspoon finely grated fresh ginger
1 clove garlic, crushed
½ teaspoon caster sugar
½ teaspoon paprika
¼ teaspoon ground cumin
¼ teaspoon ground coriander
¼ teaspoon ground turmeric
pinch chilli powder
2 x 200g single chicken breast fillets

tomato and coriander salsa
1 small tomato (130g), chopped finely
½ small red onion (50g), chopped finely
1 teaspoon sugar
1 tablespoon chopped fresh coriander

1 Combine yogurt, juice, ginger, garlic, sugar, paprika and spices in large bowl. Add chicken; turn to coat in marinade. Refrigerate 3 hours or overnight.
2 Cook chicken on heated oiled grill plate, brushing with marinade, until browned both sides and tender. Serve chicken sliced thickly, with tomato and coriander salsa, and steamed rice, if desired.

tomato and coriander salsa Combine ingredients in small bowl.
on the table in 25 minutes (plus marinating time)
serves 2
per serving 12.5g fat; 1457kJ (349 cal)
tip Chicken is best marinated a day ahead and refrigerated, covered.

chicken tikka with cucumber-mint raita

1kg chicken breast fillets
½ cup (150g) tikka paste

cucumber-mint raita
¾ cup (200g) yogurt
½ cucumber (130g), peeled, deseeded, chopped finely
2 tablespoons chopped fresh mint
1 teaspoon ground cumin

1 Combine chicken with paste in large bowl.
2 Cook chicken, in batches, on heated oiled barbecue plate until browned all over and cooked through.
3 Serve sliced chicken with cucumber-mint raita on a bed of cabbage with mango chutney, if desired.

cucumber-mint raita Combine ingredients in small bowl.
on the table in 25 minutes
serves 4
per serving 31.6g fat; 2148kJ (514 cal)
tip You can also serve this recipe in the traditional manner, by threading the chopped or sliced chicken breast fillets onto bamboo skewers before grilling or barbecuing. You will need to soak 12 bamboo skewers in water for at least an hour before use, to prevent them from splintering and scorching.

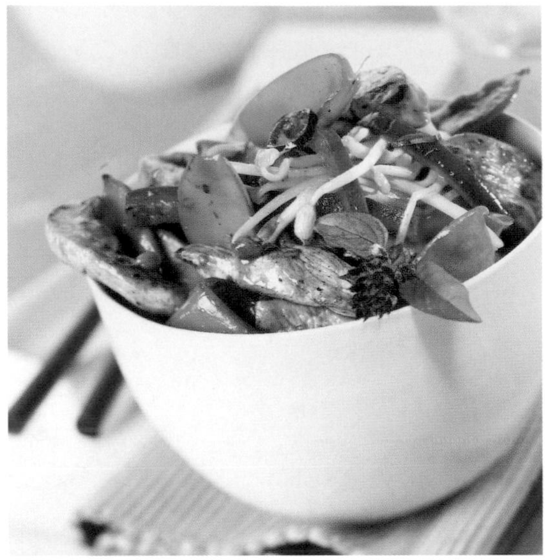

chicken chilli stir-fry

500g chicken breast fillets, sliced
3 birdseye chillies, deseeded, sliced
1 clove garlic, crushed
300g mangetout
1 large (350g) red pepper, sliced
¼ cup (60ml) oyster sauce
2 tablespoons sliced fresh basil leaves
1½ cups (120g) beansprouts

1 Heat oiled wok or large pan; stir-fry chicken, in batches, until browned and tender.
2 Stir-fry chilli, garlic, mangetout and pepper until vegetables are tender. Return chicken to wok with remaining ingredients; stir-fry until hot.

on the table in 30 minutes
serves 4
per serving 3.4g fat; 861kJ (206 cal)

chicken & green beans with thai basil

700g green beans
1 tablespoon groundnut oil
880g chicken thigh fillets, chopped coarsely
2 medium white onions (300g), sliced thickly
3 cloves garlic, crushed
1 teaspoon five-spice powder
½ cup (125ml) oyster sauce
2 tablespoons light soy sauce
½ cup (75g) cashews, toasted
½ cup loosely packed thai basil leaves

1 Cut beans into 5cm lengths.
2 Heat half of the oil in wok or large frying pan; stir-fry chicken, in batches, until browned all over and cooked through.
3 Heat remaining oil in wok; stir-fry onion, garlic and five-spice until onion softens. Add beans; stir-fry until beans are tender. Return chicken to wok with sauces and nuts; stir-fry until sauce boils and thickens slightly. Just before serving, stir in basil. Serve with noodles, if desired.

on the table in 20 minutes
serves 4
per serving 30.7g fat; 2353kJ (563 cal)
tip Sweet basil can be substituted for the thai basil, if unavailable.

thai-style chicken & vegetable curry

2 tablespoons finely chopped lemongrass
4 kaffir lime leaves, shredded
1 medium (350g) leek, sliced thickly
2 tablespoons thai green curry paste
500g chicken tenderloins, halved
2 x 375ml cans low-fat evaporated milk
1 litre (4 cups) vegetable stock
2 tablespoons soy sauce
4 small (360g) courgettes, chopped
300g green beans, halved
½ small (200g) chinese cabbage, chopped
350g pak choy, chopped
200g baby spinach leaves
1½ teaspoons coconut essence
2 tablespoons lime juice
¼ cup coarsely chopped fresh coriander

1 Heat oiled large pan; cook lemongrass, lime leaves and leek, stirring, until leek is soft. Add paste; stir until fragrant.
2 Add chicken; cook until browned and tender. Stir in milk, stock and sauce; simmer, uncovered, about 5 minutes or until thickened slightly.
3 Add vegetables; simmer, uncovered, until vegetables are just tender. Stir in essence, juice and coriander.

on the table in 30 minutes
serves 6
per serving 8.3g fat; 1216kJ (290 cal)

grilled chicken with green olive butter

400g baby new potatoes, sliced thickly
800g chicken breast fillets
150g baby spinach leaves

green olive butter
100g butter, softened
¾ cup (90g) pitted green olives, chopped coarsely
1 teaspoon finely grated lemon rind
1 clove garlic, crushed
1 tablespoon coarsely chopped fresh basil

1 Make green olive butter.
2 Boil, steam or microwave potato until tender; drain. Cover to keep warm.
3 Meanwhile, halve chicken fillets horizontally. Cook chicken on heated oiled grill plate (or grill or barbecue).
4 Divide potato among plates; top with spinach, chicken then green olive butter.

green olive butter Combine ingredients in small bowl.
on the table in 35 minutes
serves 4
per serving 32g fat; 2316kJ (554 cal)

cajun chicken with tomato salsa

750g chicken breast fillets, sliced thinly
¼ cup (18g) cajun seasoning
2 teaspoons grated lime rind
2 trimmed corn cobs (500g)
2 tablespoons olive oil
1 small red onion (100g), cut into thin wedges

tomato salsa
2 small plum tomatoes (120g), chopped finely
2 spring onions, sliced thinly
2 teaspoons lime juice
2 teaspoons balsamic vinegar

1 Combine chicken, seasoning and rind in large bowl; mix well. Cut kernels from corn.
2 Heat half of the oil in wok or large frying pan; stir-fry chicken mixture, in batches, until cooked through.
3 Heat remaining oil in wok; stir-fry corn and onion until onion is soft.
4 Return chicken to wok; stir-fry until hot.
5 Serve chicken mixture topped with tomato salsa.

tomato salsa Combine ingredients in small bowl; mix well.
on the table in 35 minutes
serves 4
per serving 21.2g fat; 1877kJ (449 cal)
tip Recipe best made just before serving; serve with sour cream, if desired.

lime chicken on lemongrass skewers

6 x 30cm-long fresh lemongrass stalks
⅓ cup (80ml) groundnut oil
1 tablespoon grated lime rind
¼ cup chopped fresh coriander leaves
6 chicken breast fillets (1kg)
¼ cup (60ml) lime juice
2 fresh red thai chillies, deseeded, chopped finely
⅓ cup (80ml) macadamia oil
1 tablespoon raw sugar
1 clove garlic, crushed

1 Cut 3cm off the end of each lemongrass stalk; reserve stalks. Chop the 3cm pieces finely; combine in large shallow dish with groundnut oil, rind and coriander.
2 Cut each chicken fillet into three strips crossways; thread three strips onto each lemongrass stalk 'skewer'. Place skewers in dish with lemongrass marinade; turn skewers to coat chicken in marinade. Cover; refrigerate 3 hours or overnight.
3 Cook skewers on heated oiled barbecue, uncovered, until chicken is browned all over and tender. Meanwhile, combine remaining ingredients in screw-top jar; shake well. Serve with chicken skewers.
on the table in 35 minutes (plus marinating time)
serves 6
per serving 33.6g fat; 1907kJ (456 cal)

spicy drumsticks with tomato, rocket & herb salad

20 chicken drumsticks (1.4kg)
¼ cup (25g) sumac
¼ cup (60ml) olive oil
½ cucumber (130g), halved lengthways, sliced thickly
2 medium tomatoes (300g), chopped coarsely
1 medium green pepper (200g), chopped finely
¾ cup coarsely chopped fresh flat-leaf parsley
¼ cup coarsely chopped fresh mint
50g baby rocket leaves
2 tablespoons lemon juice

1 Combine drumsticks and sumac in large bowl.
2 Heat 2 tablespoons of the oil in large frying pan; cook drumettes, in batches, covered, turning occasionally until browned and cooked through.
3 Meanwhile, place remaining oil in large bowl with cucumber, tomato, pepper, herbs, rocket and juice; toss gently to combine.
4 Serve drumsticks with salad.

on the table in 30 minutes
serves 4
per serving 34.9g fat; 1986kJ (475 cal)
tip A purple-red, astringent spice ground from berries growing on shrubs that flourish wild around the Mediterranean, sumac adds a tart, lemony flavour to dips and dressings and goes well with barbecued meat. It can be found in Middle Eastern food stores and major supermarkets.

chicken parmigiana-style

2 breast fillets (400g)
2 tablespoons plain flour
1 egg
1 tablespoon milk
1 cup (70g) stale breadcrumbs
¼ cup (60ml) vegetable oil
⅓ cup (85g) bottled tomato pasta sauce, warmed
4 slices ham (185g)
100g gruyère, grated coarsely

1 Preheat grill.
2 Split chicken fillets in half horizontally. Toss chicken in flour; shake away excess. Dip chicken pieces, one at a time, in combined egg and milk, then in breadcrumbs.
3 Heat oil in large frying pan; shallow-fry chicken, in batches, until browned and cooked through. Drain on absorbent paper.
4 Place chicken on oven tray; divide pasta sauce, then ham and finally cheese over chicken. Place under grill until cheese melts.
5 Serve with a parmesan and baby rocket salad, if desired.

on the table in 30 minutes
serves 4
per serving 28.6g fat; 2103kJ (503 cal)

smoked chicken salad with wild rice

2 cups (400g) wild rice
200g seedless red grapes
3 trimmed celery stalks (300g), sliced thinly
½ cup (60g) toasted pecans
350g watercress, trimmed
500g smoked chicken breasts, sliced thinly

lime and black pepper dressing
½ cup (125ml) lime juice
½ cup (125ml) olive oil
1 tablespoon caster sugar
¼ teaspoon cracked black pepper

1 Cook rice in large saucepan of boiling water, uncovered, until just tender; drain. Rinse under cold water; drain.
2 Meanwhile, combine ingredients for lime and black pepper dressing in screw-top jar; shake well.
3 Place rice in large bowl with grapes, celery, nuts and half of the dressing; toss gently to combine.
4 Divide watercress among serving plates; top with rice salad then chicken. Drizzle with remaining dressing.

on the table in 25 minutes
serves 6
per serving 33.9g fat; 2851kJ (682 cal)

meat

tamarind-glazed lamb rack with pak choy & orange salad

¼ cup (60ml) tamarind concentrate
¼ cup (60ml) orange juice
2 teaspoons sesame oil
1 tablespoon brown sugar
4 x 4 french-trimmed lamb cutlet racks (600g)
2 large oranges (600g)
100g pak choy
100g shiitake mushrooms, sliced thickly

1 Preheat oven to moderately hot.
2 Combine tamarind, juice, oil and sugar in small saucepan; reserve 2 tablespoons of the mixture in large bowl. Bring remaining mixture in pan to a boil. Reduce heat; simmer, uncovered, about 2 minutes or until mixture thickens slightly.
3 Place lamb on metal rack inside large shallow baking tin; brush hot glaze over racks. Cook, uncovered, in moderately hot oven about 20 minutes or until racks are cooked as desired. Cover racks; stand 10 minutes.
4 Meanwhile, segment oranges over reserved tamarind mixture in bowl. Add pak choy and mushrooms; toss gently.
5 Cut each lamb rack in half; place two halves on each serving plate, serve with salad.

on the table in 35 minutes
serves 4
per serving 15.4g fat; 1132kJ (271 cal)

tandoori lamb cutlets

12 lamb cutlets (900g)
½ cup (150g) tandoori paste
¾ cup (200g) plain yogurt

chutney
1 tablespoon vegetable oil
1 small red onion (100g), chopped finely
2 large tomatoes (500g), chopped finely
1 tablespoon lime juice
1 tablespoon sweet chilli sauce
2 tablespoons chopped fresh coriander

raita
½ cucumber (130g), chopped finely
2 tablespoons finely chopped fresh mint
¾ cup (200g) plain yogurt

1 Combine lamb with tandoori paste and yogurt in large bowl.
2 Cook lamb under heated grill (or on barbecue), in batches, until browned both sides and cooked as desired.
3 Serve lamb with separate bowls of chutney and raita. Top with thinly sliced spring onion, if desired.

chutney Combine ingredients in small bowl.
raita Combine ingredients in small bowl.
on the table in 30 minutes
serves 4
per serving 49.4g fat; 2553kJ (611 cal)
tip Lamb can be marinated a day ahead and refrigerated, covered.

lamb kofta with chilli tomato & yogurt sauce

1kg lean minced lamb
1 large onion (200g), chopped finely
1 clove garlic, crushed
1 tablespoon ground cumin
2 teaspoons ground turmeric
2 teaspoons ground allspice
1 tablespoon finely chopped fresh mint
2 tablespoons chopped flat-leaf parsley
1 egg, beaten lightly
6 pocket pitta, quartered

yogurt sauce
¾ cup (200g) low-fat plain yogurt
1 clove garlic, crushed
1 tablespoon chopped flat-leaf parsley

chilli tomato sauce
¼ cup (60ml) tomato sauce
¼ cup (60ml) chilli sauce

1 Using hands, combine lamb, onion, garlic, spices, herbs and egg in large bowl; divide mixture into 18 pieces and mould around skewers to form sausage shapes. Cook, in batches, under heated grill (or on barbecue) until browned all over and cooked through.
2 Serve kofta with pitta, yogurt sauce and chilli tomato sauce. Serve with tabbouleh, if desired.

yogurt sauce Combine ingredients in small bowl.
chilli tomato sauce Combine sauces in small bowl.
on the table in 30 minutes
serves 6
per serving 14.5g fat; 1817kJ (435 cal)
tips You will need 18 bamboo skewers for this recipe. Soak skewers in water for at least an hour before use, to prevent them from splintering or scorching.
Kofta can be finger-, ball- or torpedo-shaped.

lamb, spinach & spiced peach salad

20g butter
1 teaspoon ground coriander
½ teaspoon ground cardamom
¼ teaspoon ground cinnamon
3 medium peaches (450g), peeled, sliced thickly
2 tablespoons brown sugar
1 tablespoon raspberry vinegar
800g lamb fillet
1 large red onion (300g), sliced thinly
150g mangetout, trimmed, sliced thinly
150g baby spinach leaves
2 fresh long red chillies, sliced thinly

raspberry dressing
120g raspberries
2 tablespoons raspberry vinegar
2 tablespoons olive oil
1 teaspoon sugar
1 teaspoon dijon mustard

1 Melt butter in large frying pan; cook spices, stirring, until fragrant. Add peach; cook, stirring, about 2 minutes or until just tender. Add sugar and vinegar; cook, stirring, until sugar dissolves. Remove peach from pan with slotted spoon; place in large bowl.
2 Add lamb to sugar mixture in pan; cook, uncovered, over low heat until browned both sides and cooked as desired. Cover lamb; stand 10 minutes then slice thickly.
3 Meanwhile, make raspberry dressing.
4 Combine lamb and remaining ingredients in bowl with peach; toss gently. Serve salad drizzled with dressing.

raspberry dressing Blend or process all ingredients together until smooth.
on the table in 35 minutes
serves 4
per serving 31.3g fat; 2303kJ (551 cal)

paprika lamb chops with greek salad

8 lamb loin chops (800g)
2 teaspoons sweet paprika
¼ cup (60ml) olive oil
1 medium red pepper (200g), chopped coarsely
1 medium green pepper (200g), chopped coarsely
2 medium tomatoes (300g), chopped coarsely
200g feta cheese, diced into 2cm pieces
1 tablespoon lemon juice
¼ cup firmly packed fresh flat-leaf parsley

1 Sprinkle chops with paprika. Heat 1 tablespoon of the oil in large frying pan; cook chops until browned both sides and cooked as desired. Cover chops; stand 5 minutes.
2 Meanwhile, combine peppers, tomato, cheese, juice, parsley and remaining oil in large bowl; toss gently.
3 Divide salad and chops among serving plates; serve with lemon wedges, if desired.
on the table in 25 minutes
serves 4
per serving 38.6g fat; 2236kJ (535 cal)

grilled lamb with fattoush

1 clove garlic, crushed
1 teaspoon sweet paprika
1 tablespoon sumac
1 teaspoon finely chopped oregano
1 tablespoon water
1 tablespoon olive oil
800g lamb fillet

fattoush
1 large pitta bread
1 cucumber (390g), chopped coarsely
3 medium tomatoes (450g), deseeded, chopped coarsely
5 trimmed radishes (75g), sliced thinly
3 spring onions, sliced thickly
1 cup coarsely chopped flat-leaf parsley
1 cup coarsely chopped fresh mint
1 baby cos lettuce, torn
2 tablespoons sumac
⅓ cup (80ml) lemon juice
¼ cup (60ml) olive oil

1 Combine garlic, paprika, sumac, oregano, the water and oil in medium bowl; add lamb, turn to coat in mixture.
2 Cook lamb under heated grill (or on barbecue) until browned both sides and cooked as desired. Cover lamb; stand 10 minutes then slice thickly.
3 Meanwhile, make fattoush.
4 Serve lamb with fattoush.

fattoush Split pitta bread in half; toast pitta under preheated grill. Combine cucumber, tomato, radish, onion, herbs and lettuce in large bowl. Place sumac, juice and oil in screw-top jar; shake well. Pour dressing over salad; toss gently. Break pitta into small pieces over salad just before serving.
on the table in 35 minutes
serves 4
per serving 36.8g fat; 2437kJ (583 cal)

lamb schnitzel with caper herb mash & anchovy mayonnaise

4 x 150g lamb steaks
¼ cup (35g) plain flour
2 eggs, beaten lightly
1 tablespoon milk
2 cups (140g) stale breadcrumbs
½ cup (40g) finely grated parmesan
vegetable oil, for shallow-frying

caper herb mash

1kg large potatoes, chopped coarsely
½ cup (125ml) cream, warmed
50g butter, melted
2 tablespoons baby capers, rinsed, drained
2 tablespoons finely chopped fresh chives
¼ cup coarsely chopped fresh flat-leaf parsley

anchovy mayonnaise

½ cup (150g) whole-egg mayonnaise
4 anchovy fillets, drained, chopped finely
1 tablespoon lemon juice
1 tablespoon warm water

1 Using meat mallet, pound each steak between sheets of cling film until 5mm thick. Place flour in medium shallow bowl; whisk egg and milk in separate medium shallow bowl. Combine breadcrumbs and cheese in a third medium shallow bowl. Coat schnitzels, one at a time, in flour, then egg mixture, and finally breadcrumb mixture. Place schnitzels, in single layer, on tray. Cover; refrigerate.
2 Make caper herb mash.
3 Make anchovy mayonnaise.
4 Heat oil in large frying pan; shallow-fry schnitzels, in batches, until browned both sides and cooked as desired. Drain on absorbent paper; cover to keep warm.
5 Divide caper herb mash and schnitzels among serving plates; drizzle with anchovy mayonnaise.

caper herb mash Boil, steam or microwave potato until tender; drain. Mash potato in large bowl with cream and butter; cover to keep warm. Stir in capers and herbs just before serving.
anchovy mayonnaise Whisk all ingredients in small bowl until combined.
on the table in 35 minutes
serves 4
per serving 70.4g fat; 4615kJ (1104 cal)

veal steaks with italian white bean salad

1 tablespoon olive oil
8 veal steaks (680g)
½ cup (125ml) beef stock
60g butter

italian white bean salad
100g baby rocket leaves
1 large tomato (250g), chopped coarsely
½ cup firmly packed basil leaves, torn
2 x 400g cans white beans, rinsed, drained
1 tablespoon finely chopped fresh chives
¼ cup (60ml) lemon juice
2 cloves garlic, crushed
¼ cup (60ml) olive oil

1 Make the Italian white bean salad.
2 Heat oil in large non-stick frying pan; cook steaks, in batches, until browned both sides and cooked as desired. Cover to keep warm.
3 Pour stock into same pan; bring to a boil, stirring. Add butter, stir until butter melts. Reduce heat; simmer, stirring, 2 minutes. Serve steak, drizzled with sauce, with Italian white bean salad.

italian white bean salad Combine rocket, tomato, basil and beans in large bowl. Combine chives, juice, garlic and oil in screw-top jar; shake well. Pour dressing over salad; toss gently to combine.
on the table in 25 minutes
serves 4
per serving 36.6g fat; 2450kJ (585 cal)
tip Any variety of canned white beans are suitable, including cannellini, butter and haricot.

mustard veal with polenta & spinach purée

⅓ cup (95g) wholegrain mustard
2 tablespoons coarsely chopped fresh oregano
2 cloves garlic, crushed
4 veal chops (600g)
4 large plum tomatoes (360g), halved
2 cups (500ml) water
1 teaspoon salt
1 cup (170g) polenta
¾ cup (180ml) skimmed milk
¼ cup (20g) finely grated parmesan cheese
2kg spinach, trimmed
2 cloves garlic, crushed, extra
2 anchovy fillets, drained
2 tablespoons lemon juice
¼ cup (60ml) beef stock

1 Combine mustard, oregano and garlic in small bowl; brush both sides of veal with mustard mixture.
2 Cook veal and tomato, in batches, under heated grill (or on barbecue) until veal is browned both sides and cooked as desired and tomato is tender.
3 Meanwhile, bring combined water and salt to a boil in medium saucepan. Stir in polenta; cook, stirring, about 10 minutes or until polenta thickens. Stir in milk; cook, stirring, about 5 minutes or until polenta thickens. Stir in cheese.
4 Boil, steam or microwave spinach until just wilted; squeeze out excess liquid. Blend or process spinach with remaining ingredients until puréed.
5 Serve chops with tomato, polenta and spinach purée.
on the table in 35 minutes
serves 4
per serving 7.3g fat; 1626kJ (389 cal)
tip Fresh rosemary or thyme can be substituted for the oregano.

steaks with parsnip potato mash

4 sirloin steaks (880g)
½ cup (125ml) plum sauce
⅓ cup (80ml) tomato sauce
⅓ cup (80ml) Worcestershire sauce
2 cloves garlic, crushed
2 spring onions, chopped finely
1kg potatoes, chopped coarsely
2 medium parsnips (250g), chopped coarsely
40g butter, chopped
⅓ cup (80ml) cream
250g baby spinach leaves

1 Combine steaks in large bowl with sauces, garlic and onion; toss to coat steaks all over in marinade. Cover; refrigerate 30 minutes.
2 Meanwhile, boil, steam or microwave potato and parsnip together until just tender; drain. Mash with butter and cream in large bowl until smooth. Cover to keep warm.
3 Drain steaks; discard marinade. Cook steaks under heated grill (or on barbecue) until browned both sides and cooked as desired.
4 Boil, steam or microwave spinach until just wilted; drain. Serve steaks with parsnip potato mash and spinach.

on the table in 30 minutes (plus marinating time)
serves 4
per serving 37.7g fat; 3475kJ (830 cal)

teriyaki steak

750g piece rump steak, sliced thinly
¼ cup (60ml) rice vinegar
¼ cup (60ml) kecap manis
1 tablespoon brown sugar
¼ cup (60ml) lime juice
1 clove garlic, crushed
2 small fresh red chillies, deseeded, chopped finely
1 teaspoon sesame oil
1 tablespoon groundnut oil
1 large carrot (180g), cut into matchsticks
200g cabbage, shredded finely
¼ cup (50g) japanese pickled cucumber

1 Combine steak, vinegar, kecap manis, sugar, juice, garlic, chilli and sesame oil in large bowl, cover; refrigerate 3 hours or overnight. Drain steak; reserve marinade.
2 Heat groundnut oil in wok or large frying pan; stir-fry steak, in batches, until browned all over. Cover steak to keep warm.
3 Pour reserved marinade into wok; bring to a boil. Boil, uncovered, until sauce reduces by a third. Divide combined carrot and cabbage among serving plates; top with steak, drizzle with sauce. Serve with pickles and steamed rice.

on the table in 20 minutes (plus marinating time)
serves 4
per serving 18.6g fat; 1636kJ (391 cal)
tips Japanese pickled cucumber has a sour taste and is available, packaged in brine, from most Asian food stores.

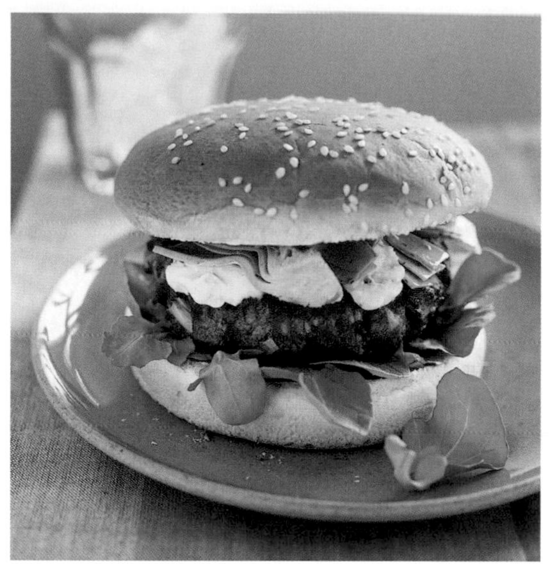

hamburger with a twist

80g gorgonzola cheese, crumbled
¼ cup (60g) soured cream
400g minced beef
120g sausagemeat
1 small brown onion (80g), chopped finely
1 tablespoon barbecue sauce
2 teaspoons worcestershire sauce
½ cup (75g) drained sun-dried tomatoes in oil, chopped finely
4 hamburger buns
50g baby rocket leaves
170g marinated artichoke hearts, drained, quartered

1 Blend or process half of the cheese with the cream until smooth. Stir in remaining cheese.
2 Using hands, combine minced beef, sausagemeat, onion, sauces and tomato in medium bowl; shape mixture into four hamburger patties.
3 Cook patties in large lightly oiled heated frying pan until browned both sides and cooked through.
4 Meanwhile, halve buns; toast, cut-side up. Sandwich rocket, patties, gorgonzola cream and artichoke in toasted buns.

on the table in 25 minutes
serves 4
per serving 30.8g fat; 2954kJ (706 cal)

beef salad with blue-cheese dressing

500g baby new potatoes, quartered
1 tablespoon olive oil
4 fillet steaks (500g)
300g green beans, trimmed, halved crossways
200g cherry tomatoes, halved
100g baby rocket leaves

blue-cheese dressing
¼ cup (60ml) olive oil
2 cloves garlic, crushed
¼ cup (60ml) orange juice
60g blue cheese, crumbled

1 Preheat oven to very hot. Place potato, in single layer, in large shallow baking tin; drizzle with oil. Roast, uncovered, about 20 minutes or until lightly browned and tender.
2 Combine ingredients for blue-cheese dressing in screw-top jar; shake well.
3 Cook steaks under heated grill (or on barbecue) until browned both sides and cooked as desired. Cover; stand 5 minutes.
4 Meanwhile, boil, steam or microwave beans until just tender; drain.
5 Slice steak thinly. Combine steak, beans and potato in large bowl with tomato and rocket, drizzle with dressing; toss gently to combine.

on the table in 25 minutes
serves 4
per serving 31.9g fat; 2143kJ (512 cal)

thai char-grilled beef salad

600g piece rump steak
2 teaspoons sesame oil
⅓ cup (80ml) kecap manis
1 cup loosely packed fresh mint leaves
1 cup loosely packed fresh coriander leaves
½ cup loosely packed fresh thai basil leaves
6 spring onions, sliced thinly
5 shallots (60g), sliced thinly
250g cherry tomatoes, halved
1 cucumber (400g), deseeded, sliced thinly
10 kaffir lime leaves, shredded finely
100g mixed salad leaves

sweet and sour dressing
½ cup (125ml) lime juice
¼ cup (60ml) fish sauce
2 teaspoons sugar
2 fresh red thai chillies, sliced thinly

1 Place steak in shallow dish; brush all over with combined oil and kecap manis. Cover; refrigerate 30 minutes.
2 Meanwhile, combine herbs, onion, shallot, tomato and cucumber in large bowl; toss gently to combine.
3 Make sweet and sour dressing.
4 Cook steak on heated oiled grill plate (or grill or barbecue) until charred lightly and cooked as desired. Stand, covered, 10 minutes; slice thinly.
5 Place steak, lime leaves and salad leaves in bowl with herb mixture. Add sweet and sour dressing; toss gently to combine.

sweet and sour dressing Combine ingredients in screw-top jar; shake well.
on the table in 25 minutes (plus refrigeration and standing time)
serves 4
per serving 12.8g fat; 1275kJ (305 cal)
tips Thai basil, also known as horapa, has a sweet licorice flavour; it is one of the basic flavours that typify Thai cuisine.
Rib-eye, boneless sirloin or eye fillet steaks are all good substitutes for rump in this recipe.

stir-fried mexican beef

750g beef eye fillet, sliced thinly
35g packet taco seasoning
1 tablespoon groundnut oil
1 large (300g) red onion, sliced thinly
1 medium (200g) red pepper, sliced thinly
1 medium (200g) yellow pepper, sliced thinly
4 small (520g) tomatoes, deseeded, sliced
2 tablespoons fresh coriander leaves

1 Combine beef and seasoning in medium bowl. Heat half the oil in wok or large pan; stir-fry beef mixture and onion, in batches, until well browned.
2 Heat remaining oil in wok, stir-fry peppers until just tender.
3 Return beef mixture to wok with tomato and coriander; stir-fry until hot.

on the table in 30 minutes
serves 4
per serving 13.4g fat; 1449kJ (346 cal)
tip You can use rib eye, rump, sirloin or topside in this recipe, if desired.

chilli beef stir-fry

4 fresh long red chillies, sliced thinly
3cm piece fresh ginger (15g), chopped coarsely
1 small red onion (100g), chopped coarsely
⅓ cup (75g) firmly packed brown sugar
1 tablespoon fish sauce
2 tablespoons vegetable oil
650g beef strips
6 spring onions, cut into 5cm lengths
450g chinese cabbage, chopped coarsely
1 tablespoon fish sauce, extra
¼ cup firmly packed thai basil leaves

1 Blend or process chilli, ginger, red onion, sugar, sauce and oil until mixture forms a coarse paste. Stir-fry chilli mixture in heated oiled wok until fragrant. Add beef; stir-fry until browned.
2 Add spring onion and chinese cabbage to wok; stir-fry until cabbage wilts. Add extra sauce and basil; stir-fry until hot. Serve with steamed rice, if you like.

on the table in 30 minutes
serves 4
per serving 20.4g fat; 1818kJ (435 cal)

gingered pork with vegetables

700g pork fillets, sliced thinly
2 tablespoons grated fresh ginger
¼ cup chopped fresh coriander
2 tablespoons rice vinegar
2 tablespoons groundnut oil
125g fresh baby corn, halved lengthways
1 medium red pepper (200g), sliced thinly
100g mangetout, halved
2 tablespoons light soy sauce
250g spinach, trimmed
3 cups (240g) beansprouts
½ cup fresh coriander leaves, extra

1 Combine pork in medium bowl with ginger, coriander and vinegar. Cover; marinate in refrigerator 3 hours or overnight.
2 Heat half of the oil in wok or large frying pan; stir-fry pork mixture, in batches, until pork is browned and cooked through.
3 Heat remaining oil in same wok. Stir-fry corn, pepper and mangetout until just tender; remove from wok. Return pork to wok with soy sauce; stir-fry until heated through. Just before serving, return cooked vegetables to wok and gently toss with pork, spinach, sprouts and extra coriander until spinach just wilts.
on the table in 25 minutes (plus marinating time)
serves 4
per serving 13.8g fat, 1443kJ (345 cal)

chilli pork with oyster sauce

1 tablespoon groundnut oil
450g pork fillets, sliced thinly
1 clove garlic, crushed
1 medium white onion (150g), sliced thinly
1 large red pepper (350g), sliced thinly
1 small green courgette (90g), sliced thinly
1 small yellow courgette (90g), sliced thinly
¼ cup (60ml) oyster sauce
1 tablespoon mild sweet chilli sauce
1 tablespoon chopped fresh coriander

1 Heat oil in wok or large frying pan. Stir-fry pork, in batches, until browned.
2 Stir-fry garlic and onion until onion is just soft.
3 Add pepper and courgettes; stir-fry.
4 Return pork to wok. Add sauces; stir-fry until hot. Serve sprinkled with coriander.
on the table in 25 minutes
serves 4
per serving 7.6g fat; 907kJ (217 cal)

spicy pork ribs

1.5kg trimmed pork spare rib slabs
¾ cup (180ml) light soy sauce
1 egg, beaten lightly
¼ cup (35g) plain flour
2 tablespoons vegetable oil
½ cup (125ml) rice wine
½ cup (100g) firmly packed brown sugar
¼ cup (50g) yellow mustard seeds
⅓ cup loosely packed, chopped fresh coriander
3 cloves garlic, crushed
1 tablespoon grated fresh ginger
3 teaspoons dried chilli flakes
1 teaspoon five-spice powder
½ teaspoon cayenne pepper

1 Cut pork into individual-rib pieces.
2 Place ribs in large saucepan. Cover with water; bring to a boil. Reduce heat; simmer, uncovered, about 10 minutes or until ribs are almost cooked through. Drain; pat dry with absorbent paper.
3 Blend ¼ cup (60ml) of the soy sauce with the egg and flour in large bowl. Add ribs; coat in soy mixture.
4 Heat oil in wok or large frying pan; stir-fry ribs, in batches, until browned all over.
5 Cook remaining soy sauce and remaining ingredients in wok, stirring, until sugar dissolves. Return ribs to wok; stir-fry until heated through. Serve with steamed rice and individual finger bowls filled with water and a few slices of lemon, if desired.

on the table in 30 minutes
serves 4
per serving 17.7g fat; 2066kJ (494 cal)
tip Ask your butcher to cut the pork ribs 'American-style' so that as much fat as possible has been removed, leaving only tender, flavoursome meat.

pork fillet with apple and leek

800g pork fillets
¾ cup (180ml) chicken stock
2 medium leeks (700g), sliced thickly
1 clove garlic, crushed
2 tablespoons brown sugar
2 tablespoons red wine vinegar
2 medium apples (300g)
10g butter
1 tablespoon brown sugar, extra
400g baby carrots, trimmed, halved
8 medium patty-pan squash (100g), quartered
250g asparagus, trimmed, chopped coarsely

1 Preheat oven to very hot. Place pork, in single layer, in large baking tin; bake, uncovered, in very hot oven about 25 minutes or until pork is browned and cooked through. Cover; stand 5 minutes then slice thickly.
3 Meanwhile, heat half the stock in medium frying pan; cook leek and garlic, stirring, until it softens and browns slightly. Add sugar and vinegar; cook, stirring, about 5 minutes or until leek caramelises. Add rest of stock; bring to a boil. Reduce heat; simmer, uncovered, about 5 minutes or until liquid reduces by half. Place leek mixture in medium bowl; cover to keep warm.
4 Peel, core and halve apples; cut into thick slices.
5 Melt butter in frying pan; cook apple and extra sugar, stirring, until apple is browned and tender.
6 Boil, steam or microwave carrot, squash and asparagus, separately, until just tender; drain.
7 Serve pork, topped with caramelised apple and sweet and sour leek, on top of the mixed vegetables.

on the table in 35 minutes (plus standing time)
serves 4
per serving 7.5g fat; 1624kJ (389 cal)

glossary

allspice also known as pimento or jamaican pepper; available whole or ground. Tastes like a blend of cinnamon, cloves and nutmeg.
arborio rice small, round-grain rice which can absorb a large amount of liquid; especially suitable for risottos.
artichoke hearts tender centre of the globe artichoke. Purchase fresh, or in brine in glass jars.
bamboo shoots the young shoots of bamboo plants; available fresh and in cans.
basil
purple also known as royal or opal basil; has an almost clove-like scent.
sweet has a strong, slightly anise-like smell and is an essential ingredient in many Italian dishes.
thai also known as horapa, is different from sweet basil in both look and taste, having smaller leaves and purplish stems Thai basil has a slight aniseed taste, and is one of the basic flavours that typify Thai cuisine.
bean thread noodles also known as bean thread vermicelli or cellophane noodles.
beans
borlotti also known as Roman beans; pale pink with darker red spots, eaten fresh or dried.
butterbeans cans labelled butter beans are, in fact, cannellini beans. Confusingly butter is also another name for lima beans, sold both dried and canned; a large beige bean having a mealy texture and mild taste.
kidney medium-sized red beans, slightly floury yet sweet in flavour; sold dried or canned, used in soups, stews, etc.
beansprouts tender new growths of assorted beans and seeds germinated for consumption in salads and stir-fries. The most readily available are mung bean, soy bean, alfalfa and mangetout sprouts.
cajun seasoning used to give an authentic USA Deep South spicy cajun flavour to food, this packaged blend of assorted herbs and spices can include paprika, basil, onion, fennel, thyme, cayenne and tarragon.
capers the grey-green buds of a warm climate shrub, sold either dried and salted or pickled in a vinegar brine. We use the pickled variety.
cardamom native to India and used extensively in its cuisine; can be purchased in pod, seed or ground form. Has a distinctive aromatic, sweetly rich flavour.
cayenne pepper a thin-fleshed, long, extremely hot red chilli; usually purchased dried and ground.
cheese
cheddar the most widely eaten cheese in the world, cheddar is a semi-hard cow milk cheese. It ranges in colour from white to pale yellow and has a slightly crumbly texture if properly matured.
feta a white cheese with milky, fresh acidity. Most commonly made from cow's milk, though sheep and goat milk varieties are available. Feta is matured in brine for at least a month, which imparts a strong salty flavour. Feta is solid but crumbles readily.
goat's cheese made from goat's milk, has an earthy, strong taste; available both soft and firm.
gorgonzola Originally from the Lombardy region of Italy, this creamy, cow-milk blue cheese is pierced with needles at about four weeks to encourage the mould to spread.
haloumi a firm, cream-coloured sheep milk cheese matured in brine; like a salty feta in flavour, it can be grilled or fried, briefly, without breaking down.
mascarpone a cultured cream product. Whitish to creamy yellow in colour, it has a soft, creamy texture, a high fat content and a tangy taste.
mozzarella a semi-soft cheese with a delicate, fresh taste; has a low melting point and stringy texture when hot.
parmesan also known as parmigiano, is a hard, grainy cheese. The curd is salted in brine for a month before being aged for up to two years in humid conditions.
pizza cheese a commercial blend of varying proportions of processed grated mozzarella, cheddar and parmesan.
ricotta a sweet, fairly moist, fresh curd cheese having a low fat content.
chillies available in many types and sizes, both fresh and dried. Wear rubber gloves to seed and chop fresh chillies as they can burn your skin. Removing membranes and seeds lessens the heat level.
chilli flakes crushed dried chillies.
chilli powder the Asian variety is the hottest, made from ground chillies; it can be used as a substitute for fresh chillies in the proportion of ½ teaspoon ground chilli powder to 1 medium chopped fresh chilli.
chinese cabbage also known as peking or napa cabbage, the pale green, crinkly leaves of this elongated cabbage only require brief cooking.
chinese rice wine made from rice wine lees, salt and alcohol; replace with a pale dry sherry if unavailable.
ciabatta a crusty Italian loaf.
cointreau citrus-flavoured liqueur.
coriander also known as cilantro or chinese parsley; bright-green leafy herb with a pungent flavour. Also sold as seeds, whole or ground.
couscous a fine, grain-like cereal product, made from semolina.
egg noodles made from wheat flour and eggs; strands vary in thickness.
fennel a fresh green bulb also known as finocchio or anise; eaten raw in salads and braised or fried as a vegetable accompaniment. Also the name given to the dried seeds which have a licorice flavour.
fish sauce also called nam pla or nuoc nam; made from pulverised salted fermented fish, usually anchovies. Has a pungent smell and strong taste; use sparingly.
five-spice powder a fragrant mix of ground cinnamon, cloves, star anise, sichuan pepper and fennel seeds.
flat-leaf parsley also known as continental parsley or italian parsley.
ginger also known as green or root ginger; the thick gnarled root of a tropical plant. Can be kept, peeled, covered with dry sherry in a jar and refrigerated, or frozen in an airtight container.

gnocchi Italian 'dumplings' made of potatoes, semolina or flour.
herbs we have specified when to use fresh or dried herbs. We used dried (not ground) herbs in the proportion of 1:4 for fresh herbs; use 1 teaspoon dried herbs instead of 4 teaspoons (1 tablespoon) chopped fresh herbs.
hoisin sauce a thick, sweet and spicy Chinese paste made from fermented soy beans, onions and garlic.
hokkien noodles also known as stir-fry noodles; fresh wheat-flour noodles resembling thick, dark yellow spaghetti. Rinse under hot water to remove starch and excess oil before use.
jasmine rice a fragrant long-grained rice; white rice can be substituted but will not taste the same.
kaffir lime leaves aromatic leaves of a small citrus tree bearing a wrinkled-skinned yellow-green fruit.
kecap manis also known as ketjap manis; a thick soy sauce with added sugar and spices.
lemongrass a tall, clumping, lemon-smelling and tasting, sharp-edged grass; use only the white lower part of each stem.
mangetout ('eat all') also called snow peas. Mangetout tendrils, the growing shoots of the plant, are sold by greengrocers.
mushrooms
button small, cultivated white mushrooms with a mild flavour.
chestnut light to dark brown mushrooms with full-bodied flavour. If unavailable, substitute button mushrooms.
flat large, flat mushrooms with a rich earthy flavour. They are sometimes misnamed field mushrooms which are wild mushrooms.
shiitake also known as chinese black, forest or golden oak mushrooms, have a unique meaty flavour popular in Asia. Often sold dried, soak to rehydrate before use.
mustard
dijon a pale brown, distinctively flavoured, fairly mild French mustard.
wholegrain also known as seeded. A French-style coarse-grain mustard made from crushed mustard seeds and dijon-style French mustard.
oil
groundnut pressed from ground peanuts; most commonly used oil in Asian cooking because of its high smoke point.
olive made from ripened olives. Extra virgin and virgin are the best, while extra light or light refers to taste rather than fat levels.
sesame made from roasted, crushed sesame seeds. Do not use for frying.
vegetable any of a number of oils sourced from plants rather than animal fats.
oyster sauce Asian in origin, this rich brown sauce is made from oysters and their brine, cooked with salt and soy sauce, and thickened with starches.
pak choy also known as bok choy, chinese white cabbage and chinese chard, has a mild mustard taste. Use stems and leaves. Baby pak choy is smaller and more tender.
paprika ground dried red pepper, available sweet or hot.
pine nuts also known as pignoli; small, cream-coloured kernels obtained from the cones of different varieties of pine trees.
pitta pocket bread small flat pieces of unleavened bread that separate into two thin rounds to form a pocket.
polenta a flour-like cereal made of ground corn (maize); similar to cornmeal but finer in texture; also the name of the dish made from it.
prosciutto salt-cured, air-dried (unsmoked) pressed ham; usually sold in paper-thin slices, ready to eat.
rice noodles noodles made from rice flour and water, available flat and wide or very thin (vermicelli). Should be soaked in boiling water to soften. Also known as rice stick noodles.
rocket also known as arugula, rugula and rucola; a peppery-tasting green leaf which can be used similarly to baby spinach leaves, eaten raw in salad or used in cooking. Baby rocket leaves are both smaller and less peppery.
salsa the Spanish word for sauce. A typical Mexican raw sauce is called salsa cruda; one made with green tomatoes or any combination of all green herbs or vegetables is called salsa verde.
sambal oelek (also ulek or olek) Indonesian in origin; a salty paste made from ground chillies.
scallops a bivalve mollusc with fluted shell valve; we use scallops which still have the coral (roe) attached.
semi-dried tomatoes partially dehydrated tomatoes in oil.
soy sauce made from fermented soy beans. Several variations are available in most supermarkets.
sugar snap peas also known as honey snap peas; mangetout can be substituted.
sumac a purple-red, astringent spice with a tart, lemony flavour; found in Middle-Eastern food stores. Substitute: ½ teaspoon lemon pepper plus ⅛ teaspoon five-spice plus ⅛ teaspoon allspice equals ¾ teaspoon sumac.
sweet chilli sauce a comparatively mild, Thai-style sauce made from red chillies, sugar, garlic and vinegar.
swiss chard also known as chard or silverbeet; a leafy, dark green vegetable, related to the beet, with thick, crisp white or red stems and ribs. The leaves are used raw or cooked.
tamarind concentrate a thick, purple-black, ready-to-use paste extracted from the pulp of the tamarind bean; it is used as is, with no soaking, stirred into sauces and casseroles.
teriyaki sauce a commercially bottled sauce usually made from soy sauce, mirin, sugar, ginger and other spices; it imparts a distinctive glaze brushed on grilled meat.
tomato paste triple-concentrated tomato puree used to flavour soups, stews, sauces and casseroles.
tomato puree canned pureed tomatoes (not tomato paste). Substitute with fresh peeled and pureed tomatoes.
turmeric a member of the ginger family, its root is dried and ground, resulting in the rich yellow powder that gives many Indian dishes their characteristic colour. It is intensely pungent in taste but not hot.
vinegar
balsamic authentic only from the province of Modena, Italy; aged in antique wooden casks to give the exquisite pungent flavour.
brown made from fermented malt and beech shavings.
raspberry made from fresh raspberries steeped in a white wine vinegar.
rice a colourless vinegar made from fermented rice and flavoured with sugar and salt. Also known as seasoned rice vinegar.
sherry natural vinegar aged in oak according to the traditional Spanish system.

index

conversion charts

Measures

The cup and spoon measurements used in this book are metric: one measuring cup holds approximately 250ml; one metric tablespoon holds 20ml; one metric teaspoon holds 5ml.

All cup and spoon measurements are level. The most accurate way of measuring dry ingredients is to weigh them. When measuring liquids, use a clear glass or plastic jug with metric markings. We used large eggs with an average weight of 60g.

WARNING This book contains recipes for dishes made with raw or lightly cooked eggs. These should be avoided by vulnerable people such as pregnant and nursing mothers, invalids, the elderly, babies and young children.

Dry measures

metric	imperial
15g	½oz
30g	1oz
60g	2oz
90g	3oz
125g	4oz (¼lb)
155g	5oz
185g	6oz
220g	7oz
250g	8oz (½lb)
280g	9oz
315g	10oz
345g	11oz
375g	12oz (¾lb)
410g	13oz
440g	14oz
470g	15oz
500g	16oz (1lb)
750g	24oz (1½lb)
1kg	32oz (2lb)

Liquid measures

metric	imperial
30ml	1 fl oz
60ml	2 fl oz
100ml	3 fl oz
125ml	4 fl oz
150ml	5 fl oz (¼ pint/1 gill)
190ml	6 fl oz
250ml	8 fl oz
300ml	10 fl oz (½pt)
500ml	16 fl oz
600ml	20 fl oz (1 pint)
1000ml (1 litre)	1¾pints

Length measures

metric	imperial
3mm	⅛in
6mm	¼in
1cm	½in
2cm	¾in
2.5cm	1in
5cm	2in
6cm	2½in
8cm	3in
10cm	4in
13cm	5in
15cm	6in
18cm	7in
20cm	8in
23cm	9in
25cm	10in
28cm	11in
30cm	12in (1ft)

Oven temperatures

These oven temperatures are only a guide for conventional ovens. For fan-assisted ovens, check the manufacturer's manual.

	°C (Celcius)	°F (Fahrenheit)	gas mark
Very low	120	250	½
Low	150	275-300	1-2
Moderately low	170	325	3
Moderate	180	350-375	4-5
Moderately hot	200	400	6
Hot	220	425-450	7-8
Very hot	240	475	9

ARE YOU MISSING SOME COOKBOOKS?

The Australian Women's Weekly Cookbooks are available from bookshops, cookshops, supermarkets and other stores all over the world. You can also buy direct from the publisher, using the order form below.

TITLE	RRP	QTY	TITLE	RRP	QTY
100 Fast Fillets	£6.99		Grills	£6.99	
A Taste of Chocolate	£6.99		Indian Cooking Class	£6.99	
After Work Fast	£6.99		Japanese Cooking Class	£6.99	
Beginners Cooking Class	£6.99		Just For One	£6.99	
Beginners Thai	£6.99		Just For Two	£6.99	
Best Food Fast	£6.99		Kids' Birthday Cakes	£6.99	
Breads & Muffins	£6.99		Kids Cooking	£6.99	
Brunches, Lunches & Treats	£6.99		Kids' Cooking Step-by-Step	£6.99	
Cafe Classics	£6.99		Low-carb, Low-fat	£6.99	
Cafe Favourites	£6.99		Low-fat Food for Life	£6.99	
Cakes Bakes & Desserts	£6.99		Low-fat Meals in Minutes	£6.99	
Cakes Biscuits & Slices	£6.99		Main Course Salads	£6.99	
Cakes Cooking Class	£6.99		Mexican	£6.99	
Caribbean Cooking	£6.99		Middle Eastern Cooking Class	£6.99	
Casseroles	£6.99		Mince in Minutes	£6.99	
Casseroles & Slow-Cooked Classics	£6.99		Moroccan & the Foods of North Africa	£6.99	
Cheap Eats	£6.99		Muffins, Scones & Breads	£6.99	
Cheesecakes: baked and chilled	£6.99		New Casseroles	£6.99	
Chicken	£6.99		New Curries	£6.99	
Chicken Meals in Minutes	£6.99		New Finger Food	£6.99	
Chinese and the foods of Thailand, Vietnam, Malaysia & Japan	£6.99		New French Food	£6.99	
			New Salads	£6.99	
Chinese Cooking Class	£6.99		Party Food and Drink	£6.99	
Christmas Cooking	£6.99		Pasta Meals in Minutes	£6.99	
Chocs & Treats	£6.99		Potatoes	£6.99	
Cocktails	£6.99		Quick & Simple Cooking (Apr 08)	£6.99	
Cookies & Biscuits	£6.99		Rice & Risotto	£6.99	
Cooking Class Cake Decorating	£6.99		Sauces Salsas & Dressings	£6.99	
Cupcakes & Fairycakes	£6.99		Sensational Stir-Fries	£6.99	
Detox	£6.99		Simple Healthy Meals	£6.99	
Dinner Lamb	£6.99		Simple Starters Mains & Puds	£6.99	
Easy Comfort Food (May 08)	£6.99		Soup	£6.99	
Easy Curry	£6.99		Stir-fry	£6.99	
Easy Midweek Meals	£6.99		Superfoods for Exam Success	£6.99	
Easy Spanish-Style	£6.99		Tapas Mezze Antipasto & other bites	£6.99	
Food for Fit and Healthy Kids	£6.99		Thai Cooking Class	£6.99	
Foods of the Mediterranean	£6.99		Traditional Italian	£6.99	
Foods That Fight Back	£6.99		Vegetarian Meals in Minutes	£6.99	
Fresh Food Fast	£6.99		Vegie Food	£6.99	
Fresh Food for Babies & Toddlers	£6.99		Wicked Sweet Indulgences	£6.99	
Good Food for Babies & Toddlers	£6.99		Wok Meals in Minutes	£6.99	
Great Kids' Cakes (May 08)	£6.99				
Greek Cooking Class	£6.99		TOTAL COST:	£	

Mr/Mrs/Ms ______________________________

Address ______________________________

______________________________ Postcode ______________

Day time phone ______________ Email* (optional) ______________

I enclose my cheque/money order for £ ______________

or please charge £ ______________

to my: ☐ Access ☐ Mastercard ☐ Visa ☐ Diners Club

Card number | | | | | | | | | | | | | | | | |

Expiry date ______________ 3 digit security code *(found on reverse of card)* ______________

Cardholder's name ______________ Signature ______________

* By including your email address, you consent to receipt of any email regarding this magazine, and other emails which inform you of ACP's other publications, products, services and events, and to promote third party goods and services you may be interested in.

ACP BOOKS

General manager Christine Whiston
Test kitchen food director Pamela Clark
Editorial director Susan Tomnay
Creative director Hieu Chi Nguyen
Director of sales Brian Cearnes
Marketing manager Bridget Cody
Business analyst Rebecca Varela
Operations manager David Scotto
International rights enquiries Laura Bamford
lbamford@acpuk.com

ACP Books are published by ACP Magazines a division of PBL Media Pty Limited

Group publisher, Women's lifestyle Pat Ingram
Director of sales, Women's lifestyle Lynette Phillips
Commercial manager, Women's lifestyle Seymour Cohen
Marketing director, Women's lifestyle Matthew Dominello
Public relations manager, Women's lifestyle Hannah Deveraux
Creative director, Events, Women's lifestyle Luke Bonnano
Research Director, Women's lifestyle Justin Stone
ACP Magazines, Chief Executive officer Scott Lorson
PBL Media, Chief Executive officer Ian Law

Produced by ACP Books, Sydney.
Published by ACP Books, a division of ACP Magazines Ltd, 54 Park St, Sydney; GPO Box 4088, Sydney, NSW 2001. phone (02) 9282 8618 fax (02) 9267 9438. acpbooks@acpmagazines.com.au www.acpbooks.com.au
Printed and bound in China.

Australia Distributed by Network Services, phone +61 2 9282 8777 fax +61 2 9264 3278 networkweb@networkservicescompany.com.au
United Kingdom Distributed by Australian Consolidated Press (UK), phone (01604) 642 200 fax (01604) 642 300 books@acpuk.com
New Zealand Distributed by Netlink Distribution Company, phone (9) 366 9966 ask@ndc.co.nz
South Africa Distributed by PSD Promotions, phone (27 11) 392 6065/6/7 fax (27 11) 392 6079/80 orders@psdprom.co.za
Canada Distributed by Publishers Group Canada phone (800) 663 5714 fax (800) 565 3770 service@raincoast.com

A catalogue record for this book is available from the British Library.
ISBN 978-1-903777-47-3